SPOTLIGHT ON

STYLES COLLECTION

21 Original Pieces in Baroque, Classical, Romantic, and Impressionist Styles for the Intermediate Pianist

CATHERINE ROLLIN

In the *Spotlight on Styles Collection*, 21 original pieces by Catherine Rollin are gathered in one book to serve as an introduction to the distinctive styles of Baroque, Classical, Romantic, and Impressionist music. Each piece is accessible to the intermediate pianist and features elements that are stylistically characteristic of one of these four periods. Through this collection, students are offered a fulfilling musical experience as well as preparation for the study of the masterworks.

Alfred Music
P.O. Box 10003
Van Nuys, CA 91410-0003
alfred.com

ISBN-10: 0-7390-9966-3
ISBN-13: 978-0-7390-9966-7

Cover Photo
Concert lighting against a dark background illustration: © Shutterstock.com / Skylines

Contents

Contents

Romantic Style

Impressionist Style

Suggestions & Program Notes

Baroque Style

Spirit, charm, and rhythmic vitality characterize the music of the Baroque era. In addition to a march and minuet, this collection introduces several dance forms that students typically encounter only in the advanced Baroque suites. These include the bourrée, gavotte, gigue, and sarabande. Since the use of ornamentation was second nature to Baroque musicians, trills and mordents are written out so students can easily perceive them as a truly integral part of the music.

The **bourrée** is a Baroque dance that originated in France. It is usually in a quick, duple meter and begins on the upbeat. For the bourrée on page 14, observing all articulation marks will help to produce the lively spirit that characterizes this dance.

The **gavotte** is another Baroque dance that originated in France. It is in 4/4 meter and begins on the third beat of the measure with two quarter-note upbeats. The phrases begin on the third beat and end on the second. This precise rhythmic structure of the phrasing gives the gavotte a rather dignified, stately quality. There are a few **trills** in the gavotte on page 18. A trill is the alternation between two notes. Trills typically have a minimum of four notes, and in the Baroque style, they generally begin on the note above the principal note. In Baroque music, the 𝆖 sign is usually used to indicate a trill. The musicians of the day immediately understood how to execute this sign. In this gavotte, the trills (in measures 7, 23, and 25) are written out.

The **gigue** is a dance that is most often in 6/8 meter. It has a very lively and robust character. The gigue on page 20 uses many mordents. In Baroque music, a **mordent** is indicated by the 𝆗 sign. It is usually a three-note ornament that starts on the principal note, goes down a step, and then returns to the principal note.

The **march** is a musical form that was created to keep a very steady rhythm for marching. It evolved into an important form of art music during the Baroque era. Just as it was originally intended, the march overture on page 8 should have an extremely steady and vigorous beat.

The **minuet** was one of the most popular dance forms in the Baroque period. It originated as a French country dance in 3/4 meter. It was used extensively by Baroque composers. As with most minuets, the minuet on page 16 is to be performed in a relaxed, graceful style.

Ornamentation is the embellishment of the basic melodic and/or harmonic structure of the music. The use of ornaments (i.e. trills, mordents, etc.—see above definitions) and incorporating those elements *seamlessly* into the music is one of the important skills in the performance of Baroque music.

The **sarabande** is one of the dances most commonly found in Baroque suites. It is in a slow, triple meter. As is the case with most sarabandes, the stress falls on the second beat of the measure in the sarabande on page 10.

A **suite** in the Baroque period was a grouping of pieces in the same key. This was a very popular format of the era. The suite on pages 8-13 can be performed as a set or as individual pieces.

Suggestions & Program Notes

Classical Style

The Classical period was an exciting time in the development of keyboard music. Composers were inspired by the recently invented pianoforte and all of the many creative possibilities that this new instrument provided. Also, new forms of music were emerging, particularly the sonata-allegro form, that emphasized the development of thematic material and the exploration of harmonic movement. In this collection, the sonatina, theme and variations, and Classical minuet are explored to capture the spirit of the Classical period while keeping the technical demands within the range of an intermediate pianist.

The **minuet** was a French country dance in 3/4 meter that was first introduced in the court of Louis XIV in the middle of the 17th century. It then became a standard movement in the Baroque suites and was the only form of these dance suite movements to continue to flourish in the Classical period. The minuet on page 52 is to be played with grace and dignity.

A **sonatina (piano sonatina)** is a work that is typically comprised of three movements. The first movement is fairly fast, the second movement is slower, and the last movement is usually quite quick. The outer movements are generally in the same key, which is the overall key of the piece. The middle movement is in a related but contrasting key. Both the *Sonatina in G*, on pages 24-33, and the *Sonatina in C*, on pages 34-43, adhere to these characteristics.

The first movements of both sonatinas are in **sonata-allegro form**. This was the prevailing form for first movements in the Classical period. This form has three major sections: **exposition**, **development**, and **recapitulation**. In the exposition, the thematic material is presented. Typically, there are two major themes: the first is in the tonic (I) key and the second is in a related key, usually that of the dominant (V). The two themes are also contrasting in character.

The development section employs elements of one or both of the primary themes from the exposition. It develops the initial material through use of dramatic harmonic changes or other means of exploration. In sonatinas, the development is usually shorter than that of a sonata.

In the recapitulation, the music from the exposition is basically repeated. The most important change, however, is that the second theme is now written in the tonic key. The recapitulation is often followed by a coda which is a concluding section that gives a strong sense of finality to the music. Both of the sonatinas in this collection have a coda. It is suggested that the performer analyze the music and identify the different sections described above. This will help develop an understanding of the structure and will aid in memorization.

The second movements of these sonatinas, as well as many others, have a songlike quality. They contrast with the first and third movements in key, character, and tempo. In the *Sonatina in G* and the *Sonatina in C*, the use of **finger pedaling** is suggested. This is done independently or in conjunction with the damper pedal. The performer holds the first note of each broken chord group to give a more sustained, legato sound to the accompanying figure (see footnote on page 28 for the realization of finger pedaling).

The third movements of both sonatinas are in **rondo form**. This was a popular form for final movements during the Classical period in sonatas, sonatinas, concertos, and symphonies. In this form, the rondo or A theme keeps returning after alternating with contrasting material. In these two rondos, the form is ABACA.

Theme and variations was a popular form in the Classical period. It was often used by Mozart, Haydn, and Beethoven. In the *Variations on an Original Theme* on pages 44-51, as is typical of the Classical period, the thematic material is varied, but the essential harmonies and the ternary structure of the theme are maintained throughout.

Suggestions & Program Notes

Romantic Style

In music of the Romantic era, the most important elements are expressive, cantabile melodies and full-bodied sound. These concepts are explored through the following characteristic forms: the etude, mazurka, nocturne, polonaise, and waltz.

The **etude** is a study that emphasizes a particular technical point. The etudes of Chopin created a new genre, the concert etude. These were studies that (from a musical standpoint) could also be performed publicly. The etude on page 62 is intended to develop the ability to voice with the fifth finger of the right hand. An effective practice method would be to play the inner 16th notes staccato while holding each quarter note with the fifth finger. This will help lighten the touch on the inside of the hand. In keeping with the Romantic tradition, this etude is also intended for public performance.

The **mazurka** is a Polish folk dance in 3/4 meter that tends to stress the weak beat. In the mazurka on page 57, the accentuation is generally on beat two. It is important to follow the pedaling and the articulation so this aspect of the mazurka is captured. The melodic material is simple and attempts to reflect the folk quality that infused the original mazurkas with their special spirit.

The **nocturne**, meaning "night song," was a form developed by the Irish keyboard composer John Field. The form was then brought to its greatest heights by Frédéric Chopin, who explored intimate emotions through beautiful, cantabile melodies that were often highly ornamented. In the nocturne on page 54, the ornaments are already realized in the score. The primary emphasis should be on beautiful tone and legato playing.*

The **polonaise** is a Polish national dance in 3/4 meter. It has a stately quality derived largely from the repeated ♪♬ ♫ ♫ pattern that is characteristic of the Romantic-style polonaise. In the polonaise on page 64, that particular pattern is in the left hand, contrasted with a broad melody in the right hand throughout most of the piece.

The **waltz** is a dance in triple meter with the emphasis on the downbeat. Beats two and three should always be played very lightly in the left hand for an effective waltz feel. During the Romantic period, the waltz developed into an elegant art music characterized by grace and often a bit of flamboyance. The waltz on page 60 has a simple melody in the **A** section with a trace of melancholy. The **B** section should be played with flair, which can be easily achieved by observing the correct fingering.

* Chopin often uses "fioratura" or flowery passages. These passages are usually comprised of notes that move quickly in relationship to the predominant note values in that section of the music and often also have an irregular number of notes in the right hand in relationship to the left hand accompaniment. In this nocturne, the 32nd note passages based on trills or scales serve as an introduction to fioratura figures. While "flowery," these introductory fioraturas are accessible with their even amount of notes in relationship to the accompaniment.

Suggestions & Program Notes

Impressionist Style

Impressionism refers to the French arts movement in the latter part of the 19th century and the early 20th century. The primary composer and music innovator of this style was Claude Debussy. Maurice Ravel also contributed many major impressionist works. Through the use of various harmonic devices (i.e., extended chords, whole-tone scales, augmented chords, bi-tonality, and pentatonic scales), Debussy created music that was less oriented toward a tonal center and more concerned with creating musical imagery. He also experimented with many pianistic effects to create a variety of sound and musical images. In the following pieces, a diverse palette of colors and sounds at the piano are explored to help students discover the incredible pictures they can "paint" with their two hands and some imagination.

Chouchou's Cakewalk, on page 67, is based on the cakewalk rhythm ♬ ♫ that appeared in several of Debussy's works. The cakewalk was a dance that originated in the mid-1800s by plantation slaves. Its syncopated melodies against a strict left hand were a precursor to ragtime. Chouchou was the affectionate nickname of Debussy's daughter. She was a source of inspiration for many of Debussy's playful works.

Iberia, on page 74, is influenced by the exuberance of Spanish dance rhythms. Many of Debussy's works reflect this influence. *Iberia* also uses a lot of alternating hand technique, which is a prevalent device in Debussy's piano writing.*

Under the Sea (Sous la mer), on page 70, evokes the images of the sea. Both Debussy and Ravel wrote many works influenced by water imagery. The introduction of this piece is based on a whole-tone scale. Void of half steps, whole-tone patterns are harmonically perfect to emulate the amorphous nature of water. This piece also uses seventh chords (measure 5), augmented chords (measure 27), and bi-tonality (measure 41). These harmonic devices help elicit water imagery.

Valse Noble, on page 83, and *Valse Sentimentale*, on page 86, reflect the strong influence of the waltz on the writing of both Debussy and Ravel. Sometimes it is treated adoringly and with sentiment, as in Debussy's *Valse Romantique*, and at other times it is almost mocked as the symbol of the end of an era, as in Ravel's *La Valse*. *Valse Noble* and *Valse Sentimentale* are intended to capture both the bold drama of the waltz and its delicate, whimsical side, that reaches expressive heights through extensive rubato in *Valse Sentimentale*. In *Valse Noble*, extended chords lend this romantic dance its impressionistic color.

Water Lilies (Nénuphars), on page 80, is inspired by the art works of Claude Monet. Much of the music of the Impressionist era is intended to capture visual ideas through aural imagination. The use of extended chords (sevenths and ninths) helps create these images.

Windchimes (Carillons dans le vent), on page 77, is largely based on a pentatonic scale comprised of all black keys. Both Debussy and Ravel were dedicated to introducing musical sounds and rhythms of other cultures into their music. They were influenced by the five-note pentatonic scale that was prevalent in Asian music.

* This technique is also commonly used in the keyboard works of many Spanish composers.

Suite in C

I. March Overture

Catherine Rollin

Allegro con spirito

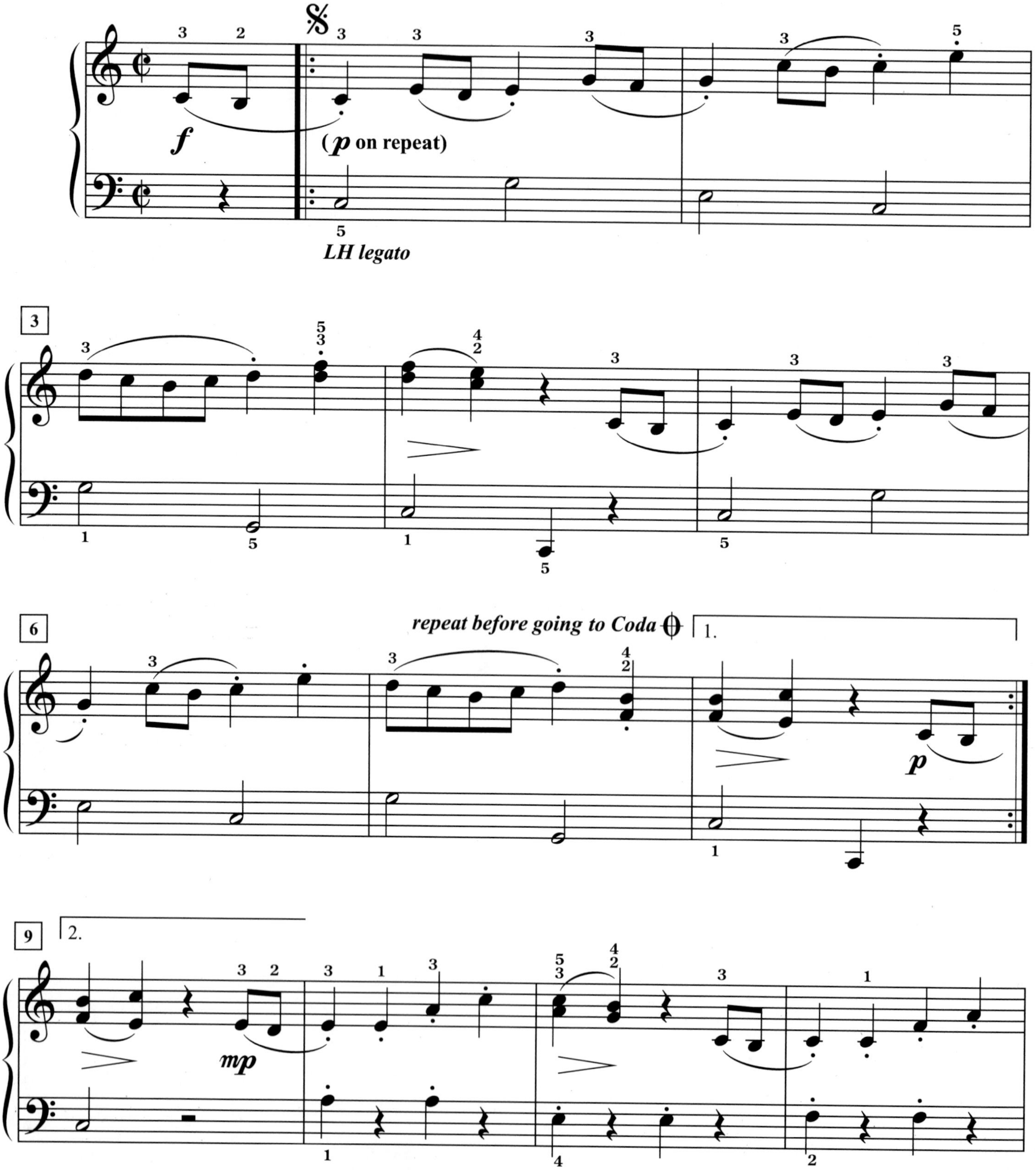
f
(p on repeat)
LH legato
3
6
repeat before going to Coda
1.
p
9
2.
mp

* The three pieces in this suite can be played individually or as a set.

13
p

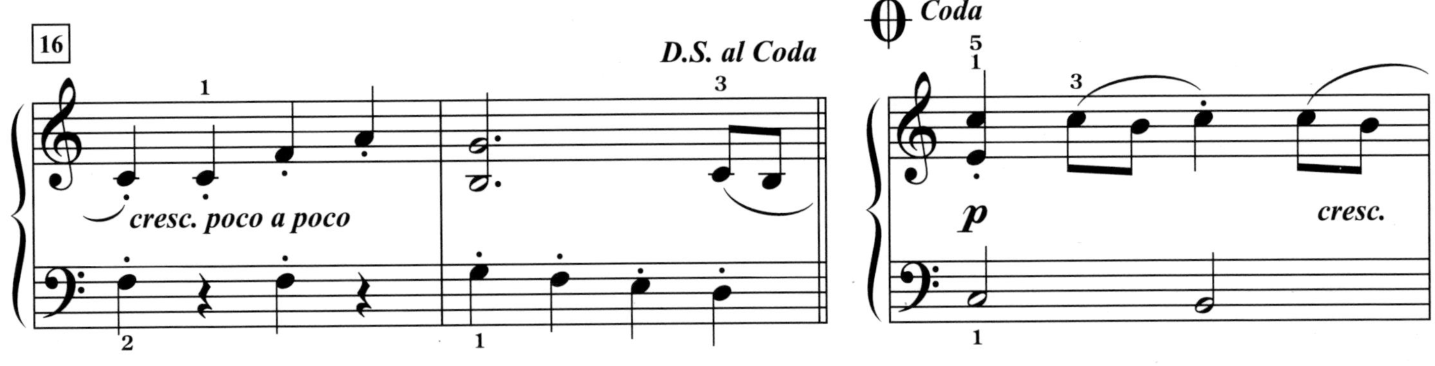
16
cresc. poco a poco
D.S. al Coda
Coda
p
cresc.

19
mp
cresc.

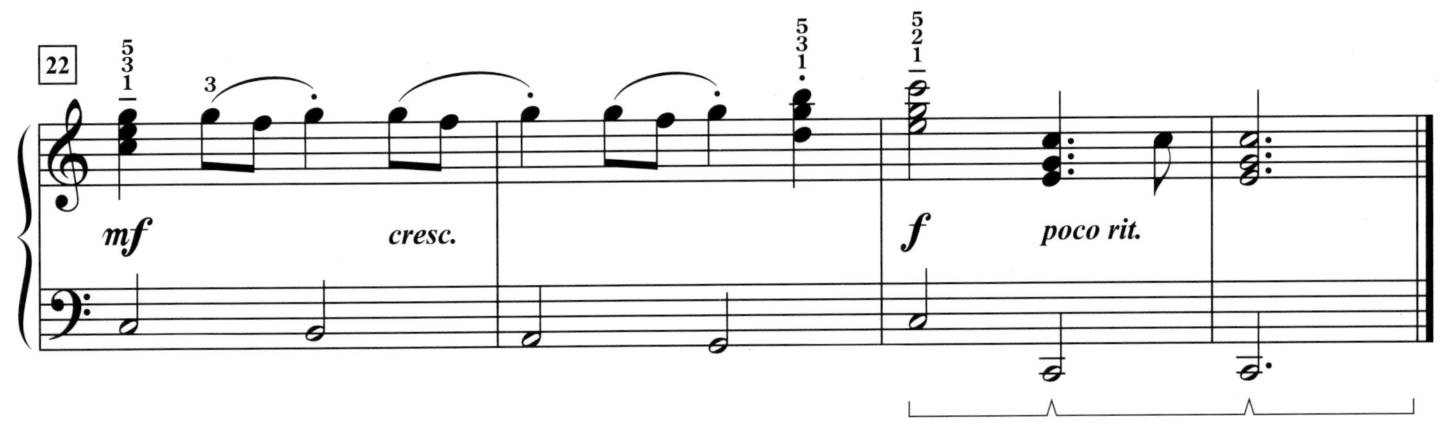
22
mf
cresc.
f
poco rit.

II. Sarabande

Catherine Rollin

III. Gigue

Catherine Rollin

* Pedals are optional

17
1
mf
1

21

25
1 3
1 2
f–p
5
2
LH over
5
2

29
1

33
1
mp
1

37

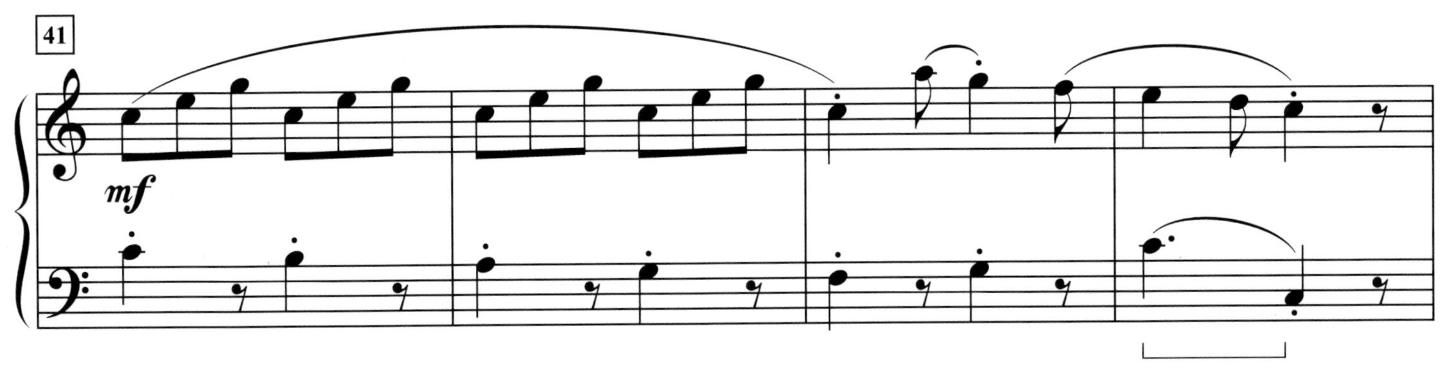
41
mf

45
4
2
cresc. e poco rit.
f

Bourrée

Allegretto con brio

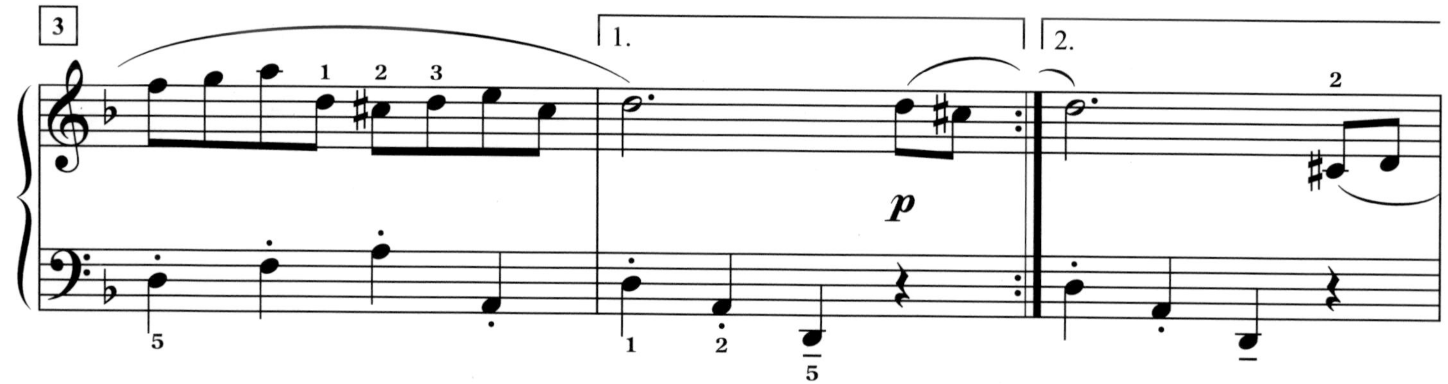

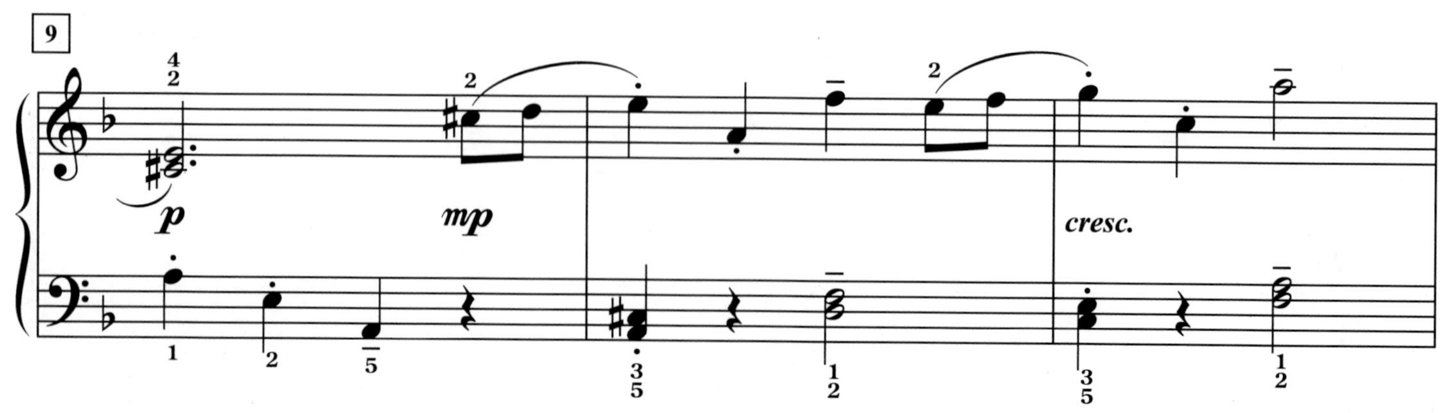

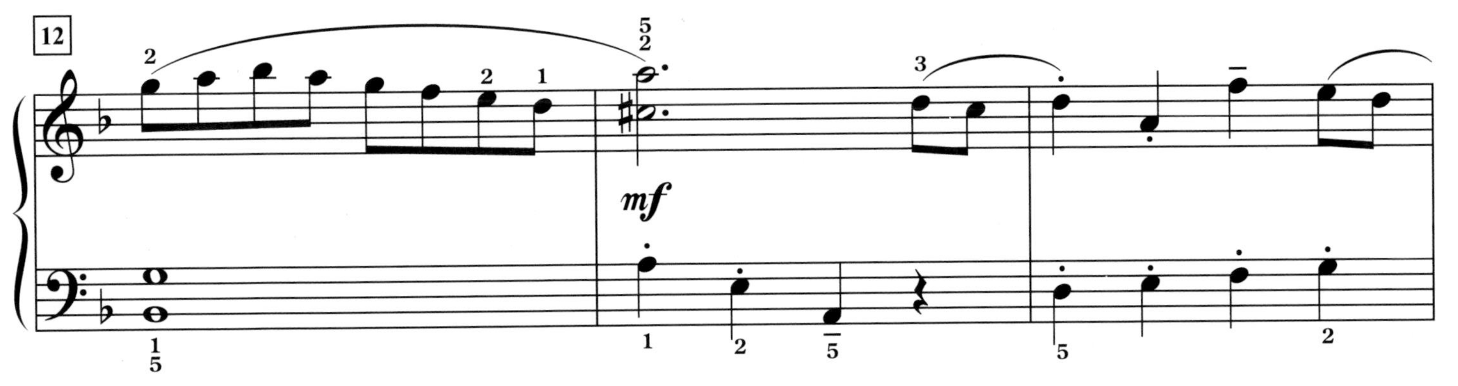
12
mf

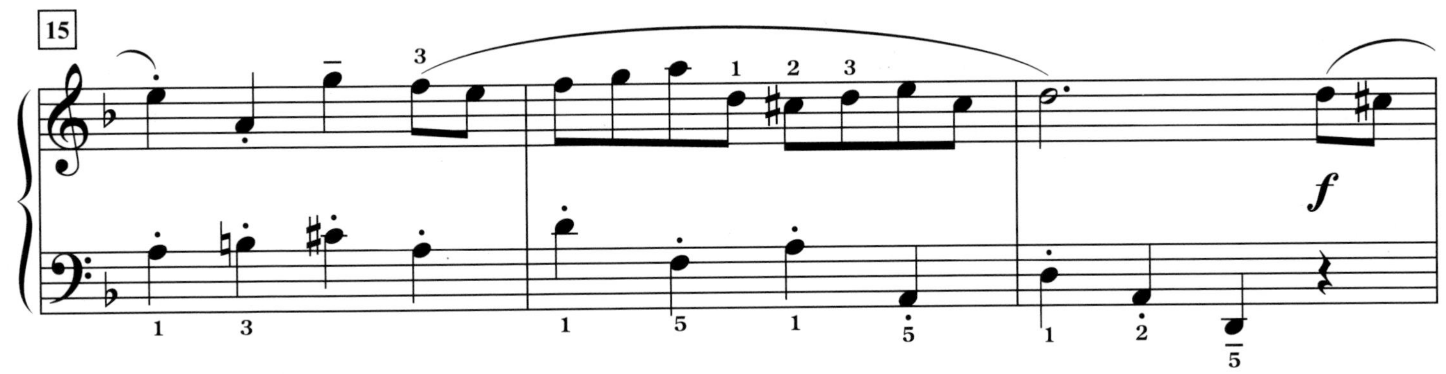
15
f

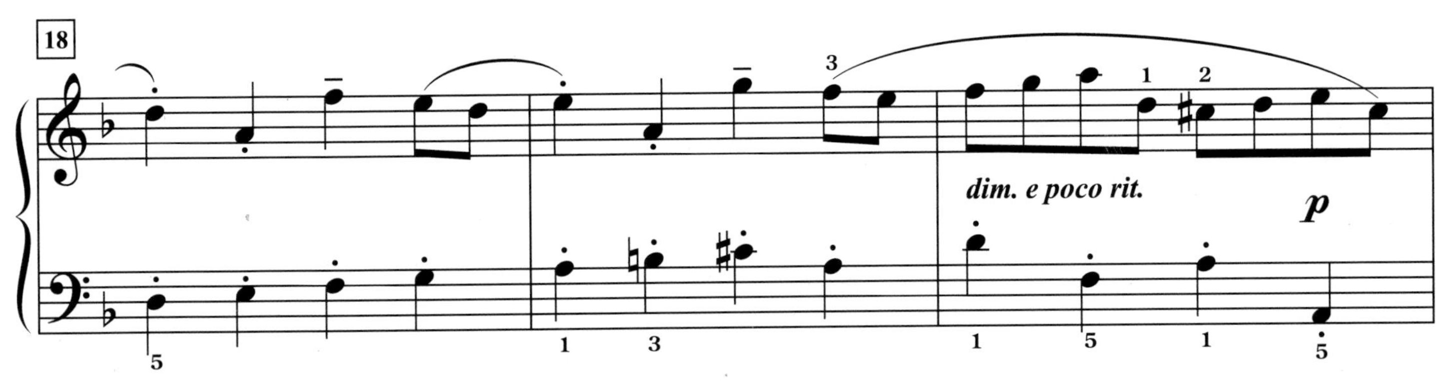
18
dim. e poco rit.
p

21
a tempo
mp
p

Minuet

Catherine Rollin

* All ascending broken triads in L.H. have a slight crescendo to shape the accompaniment.
** Staccatos to be played at approximately half the note's value (portato touch) to achieve the graceful style intended in this Minuet.

13
mf

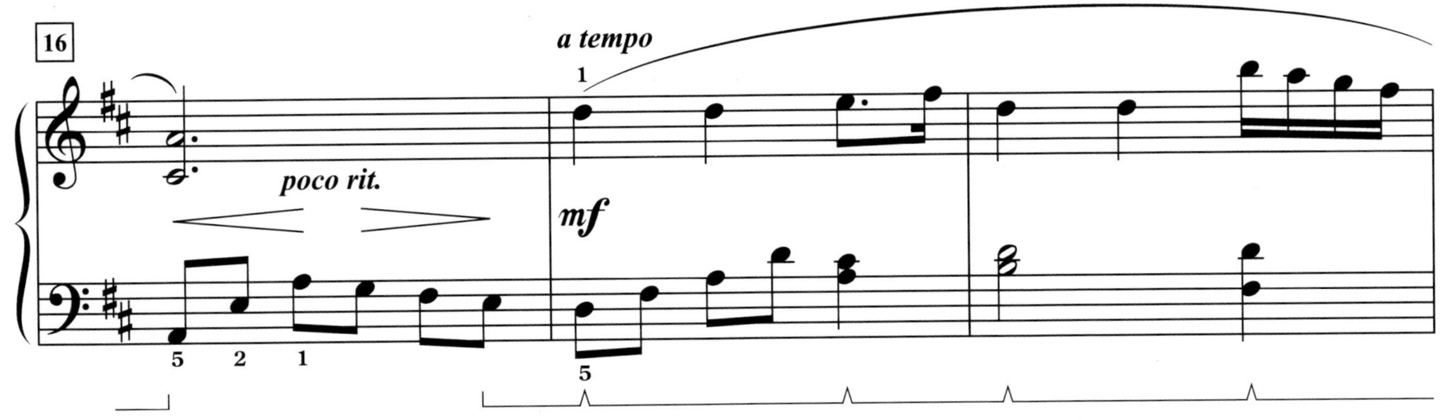
16
a tempo
poco rit.
mf

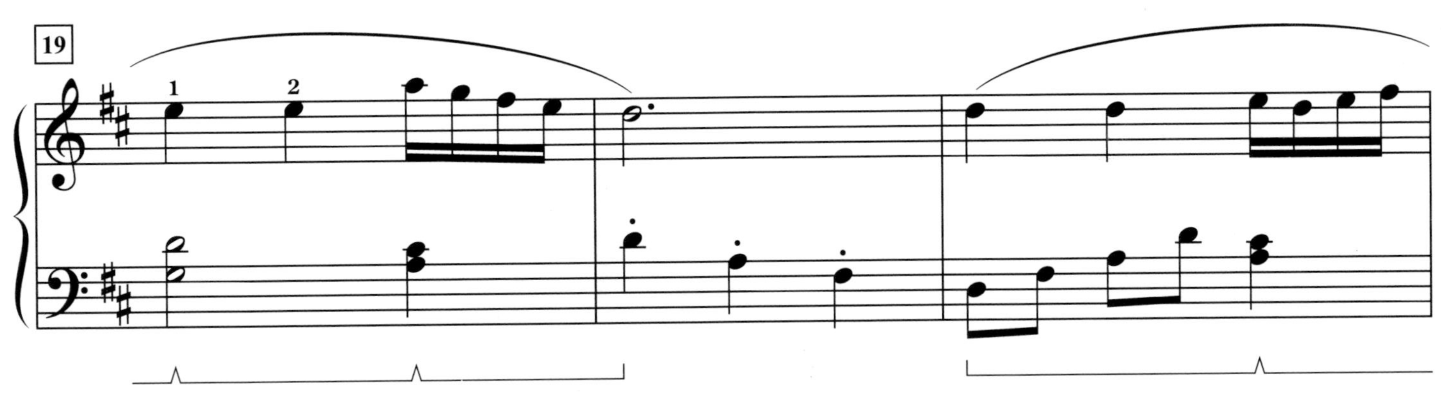
19

22
rit. e dim.
p

Gavotte

Catherine Rollin

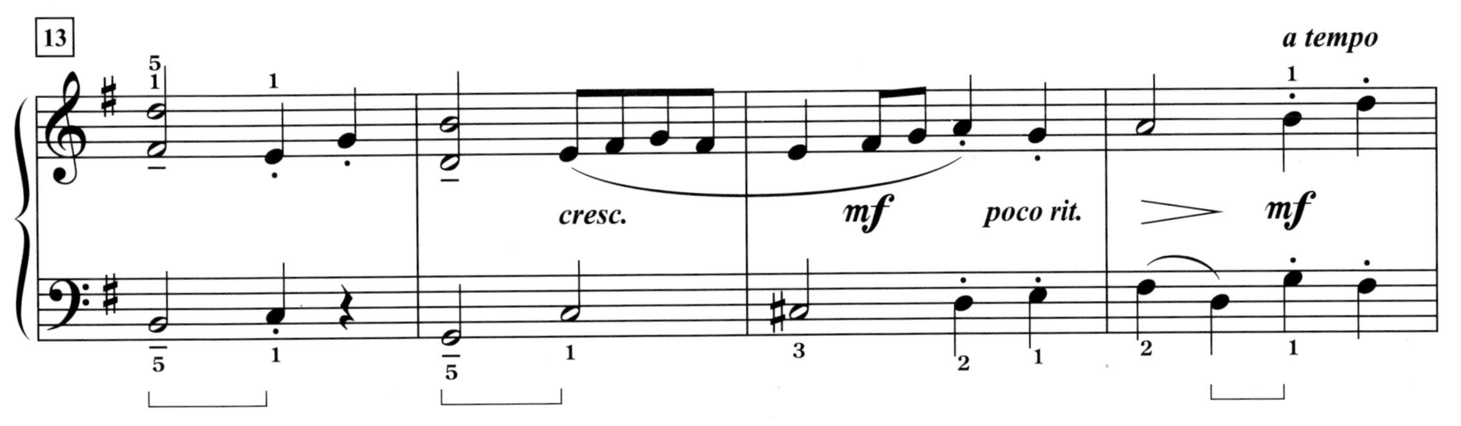
13
a tempo
cresc.
mf
poco rit.
mf

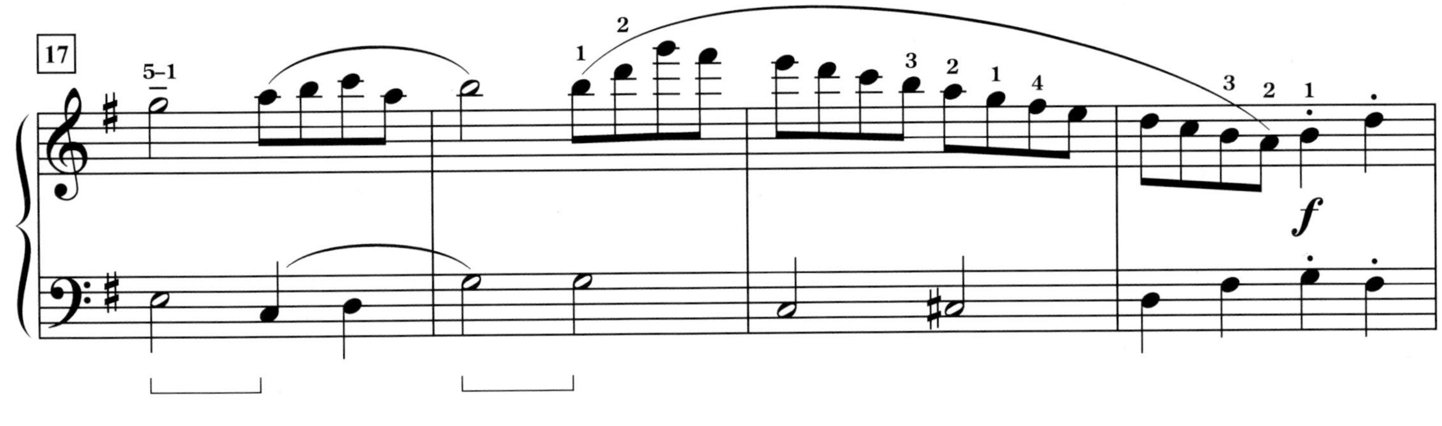
17
f

21
poco rit.

24
allargando
rit.

Gigue in D Minor

Catherine Rollin

Allegro giocoso

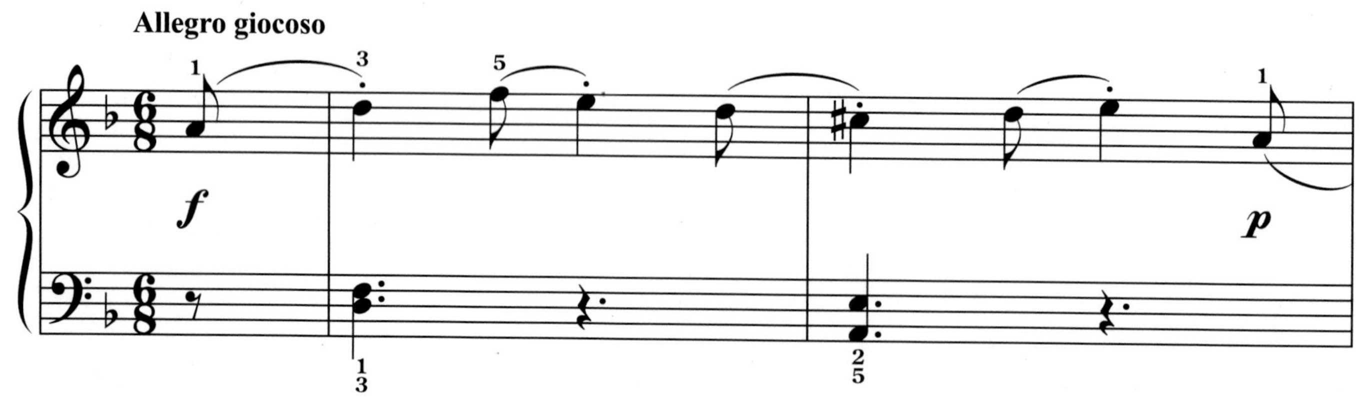

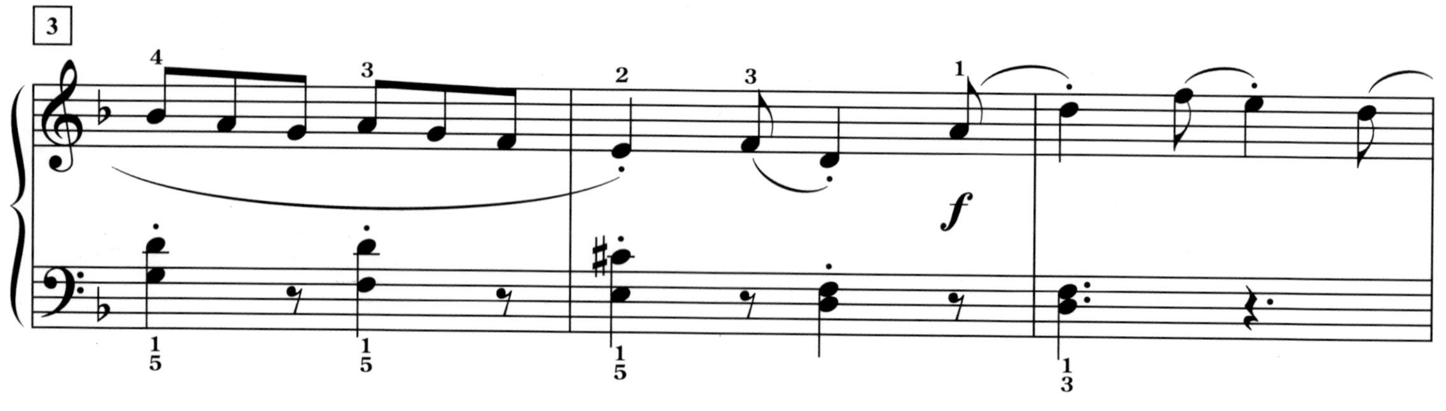

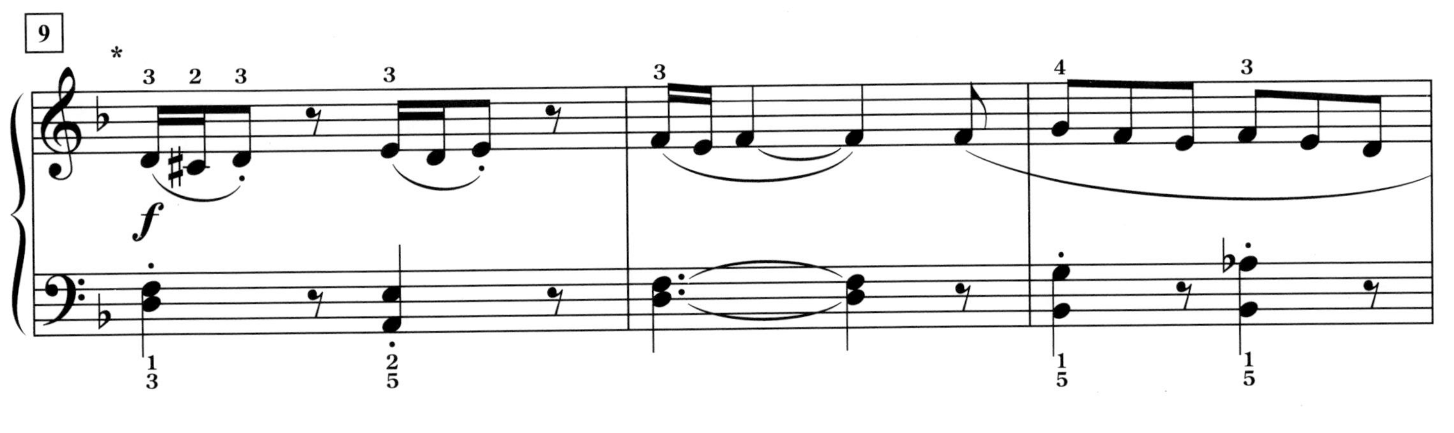

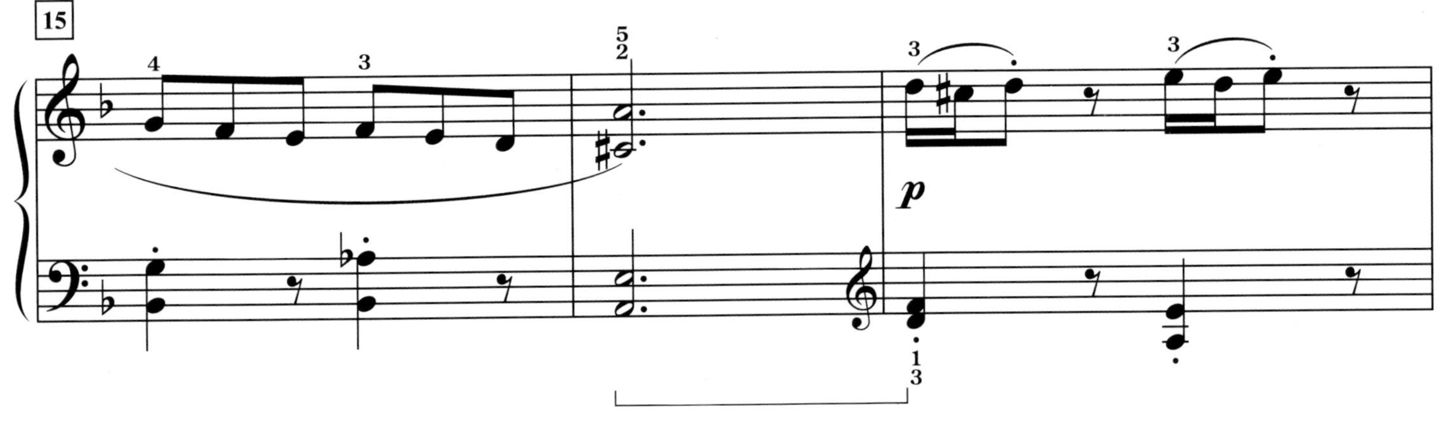

* The right hand figures are written out mordents. See program notes on page 4.

21
poco rit.

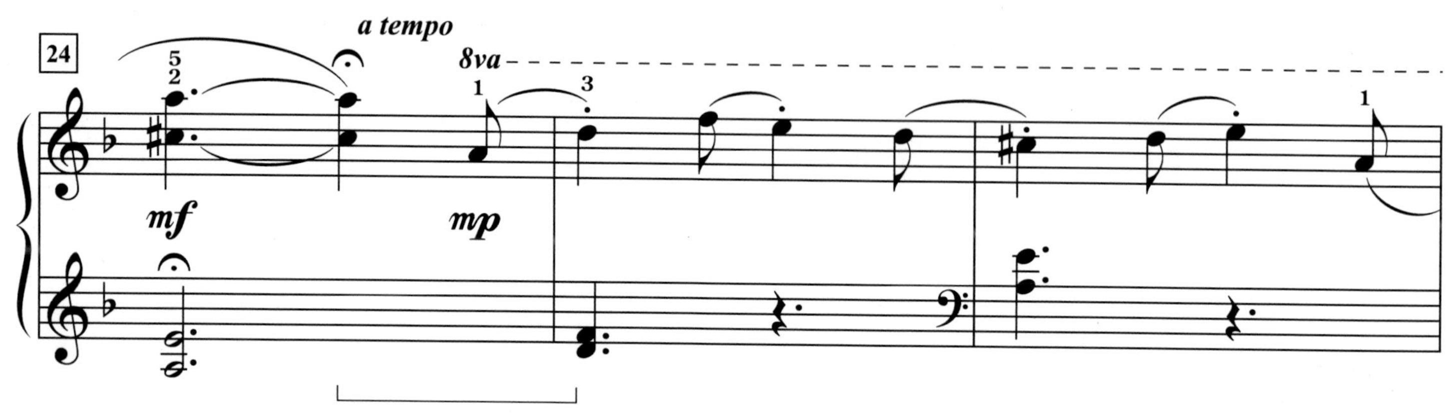
24
a tempo
8va
mf
mp

27
loco
mf

30
mp

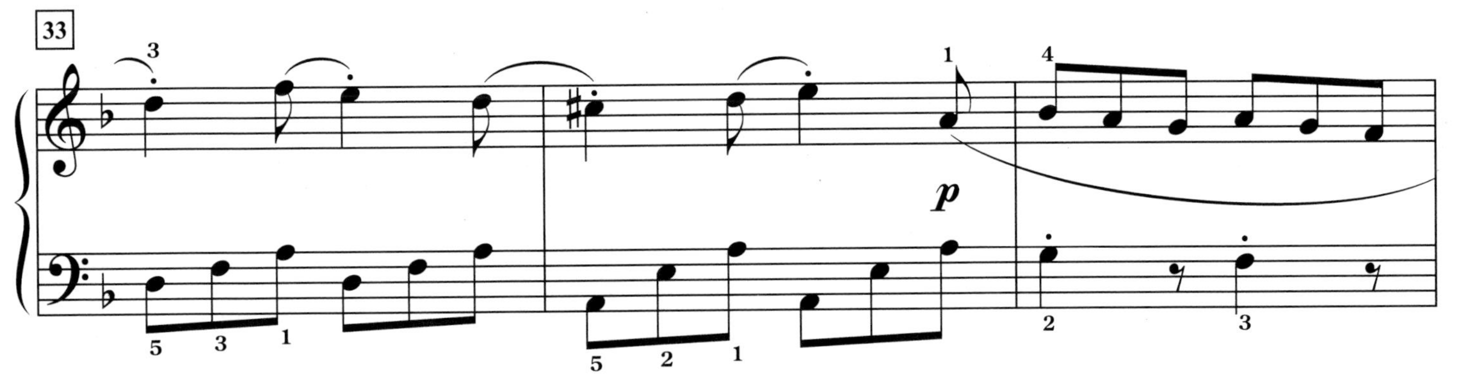
33
p

36
mf
p

39
cresc. poco a poco

42
f
mp rit.
p

Sonatina in G

I.

Catherine Rollin

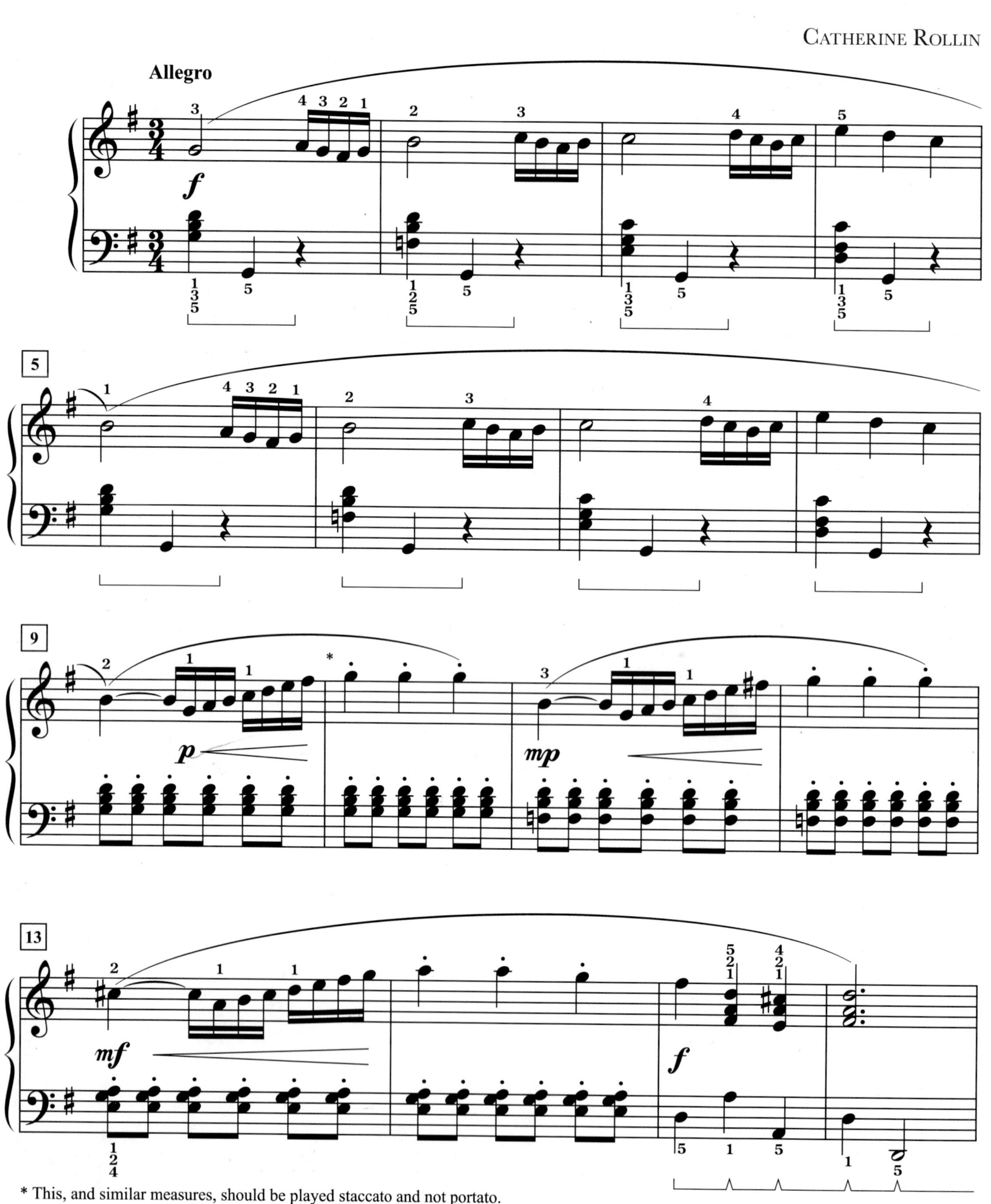

* This, and similar measures, should be played staccato and not portato.

Classical Style

* In the Classical period, the exposition was traditionally repeated. In this piece, it is the option of the performer.

37
f
rit.
41
a tempo
45
49
p
mp
53
mf
f

57
mp
cresc.
mf
61
mp
cresc.
mf
65
p
mp
mf
f
69
p
mp
mf
f
73
rit.

II.

* It is suggested that finger pedaling be used in the left hand.
This is realized as:

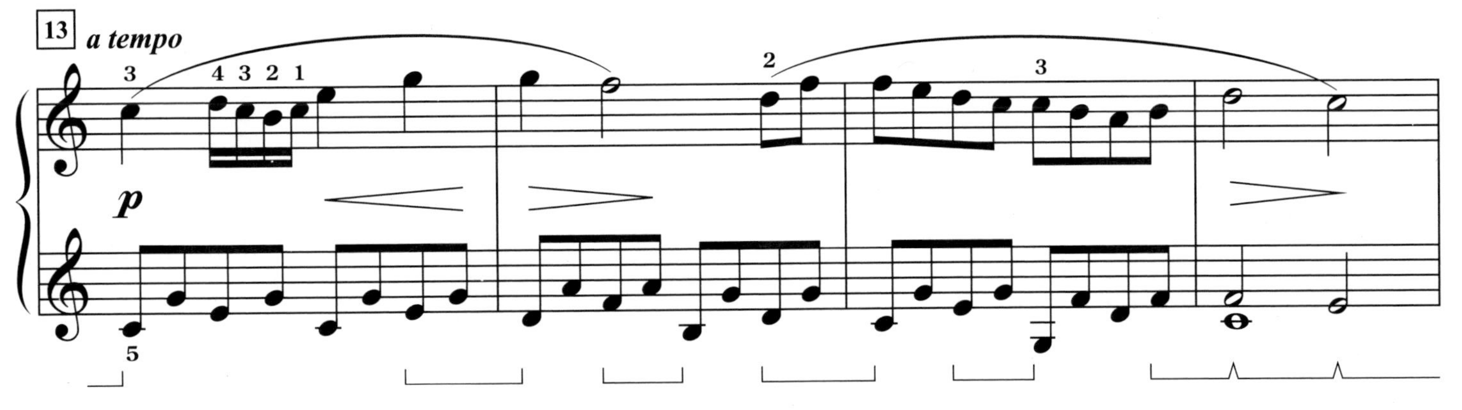
13
a tempo
p

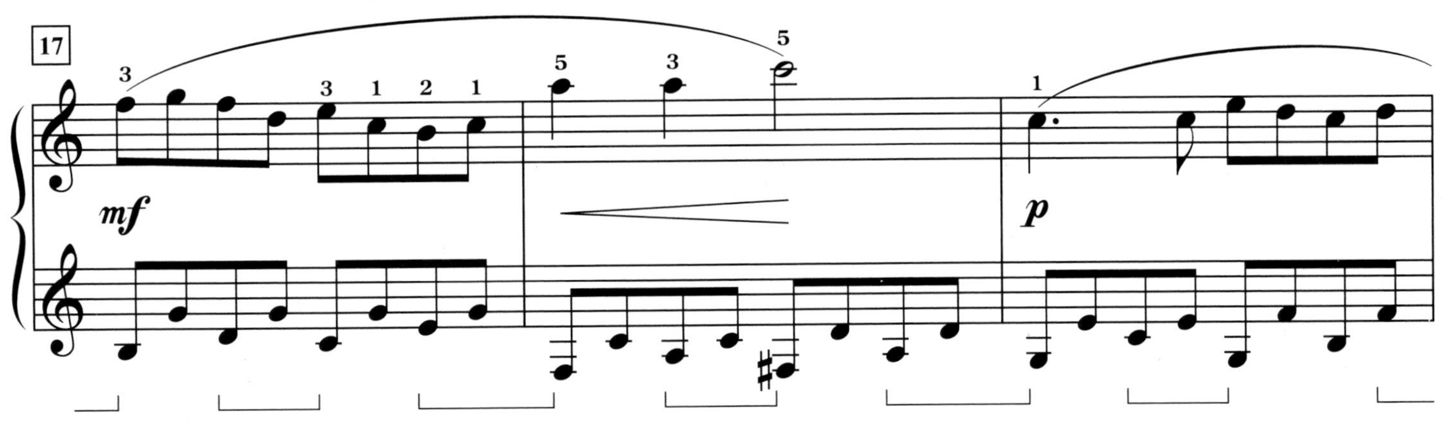
17
mf
p

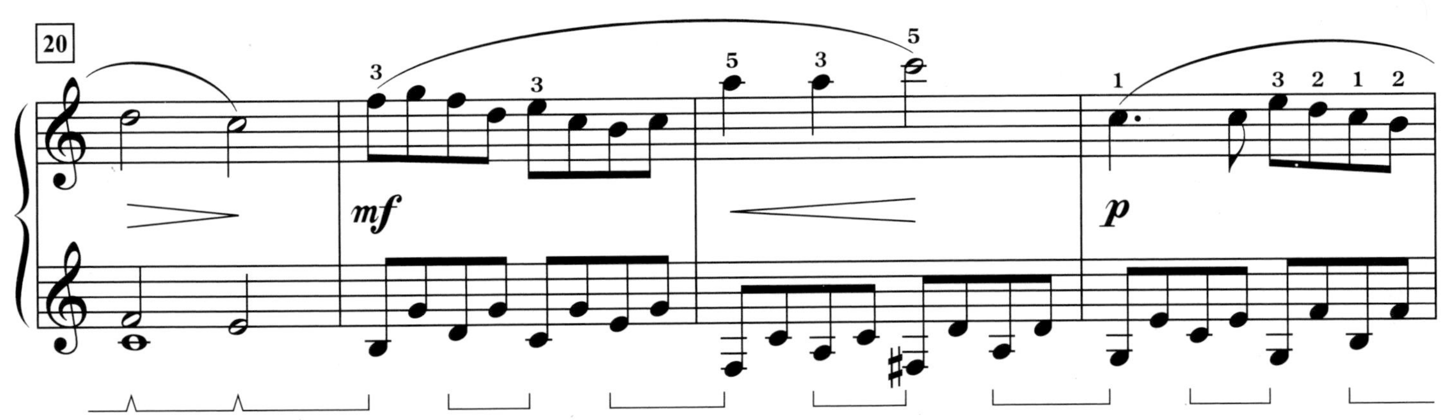
20
mf
p

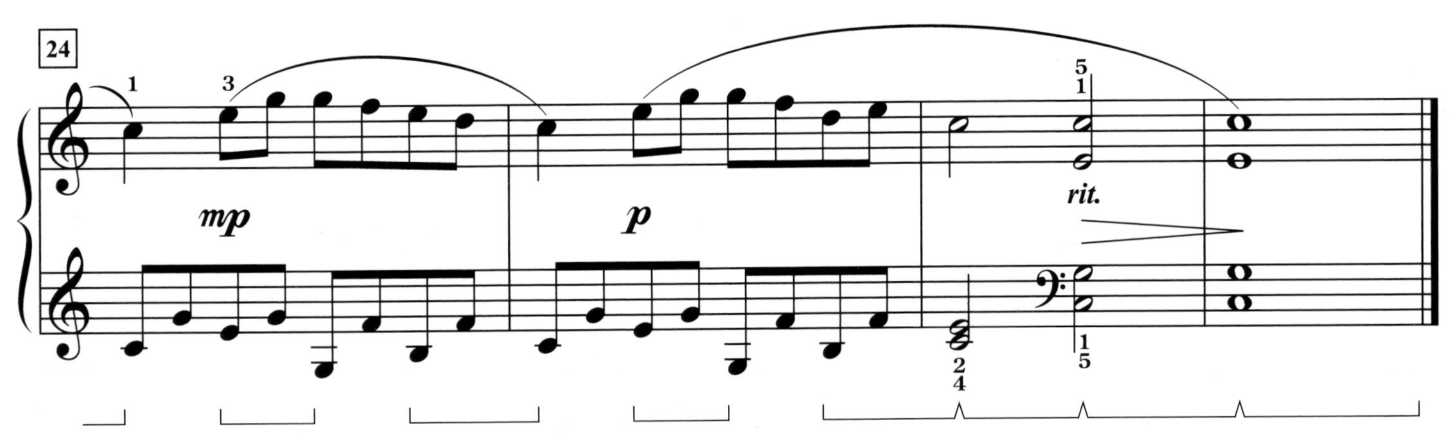
24
mp
p
rit.

III.

Catherine Rollin

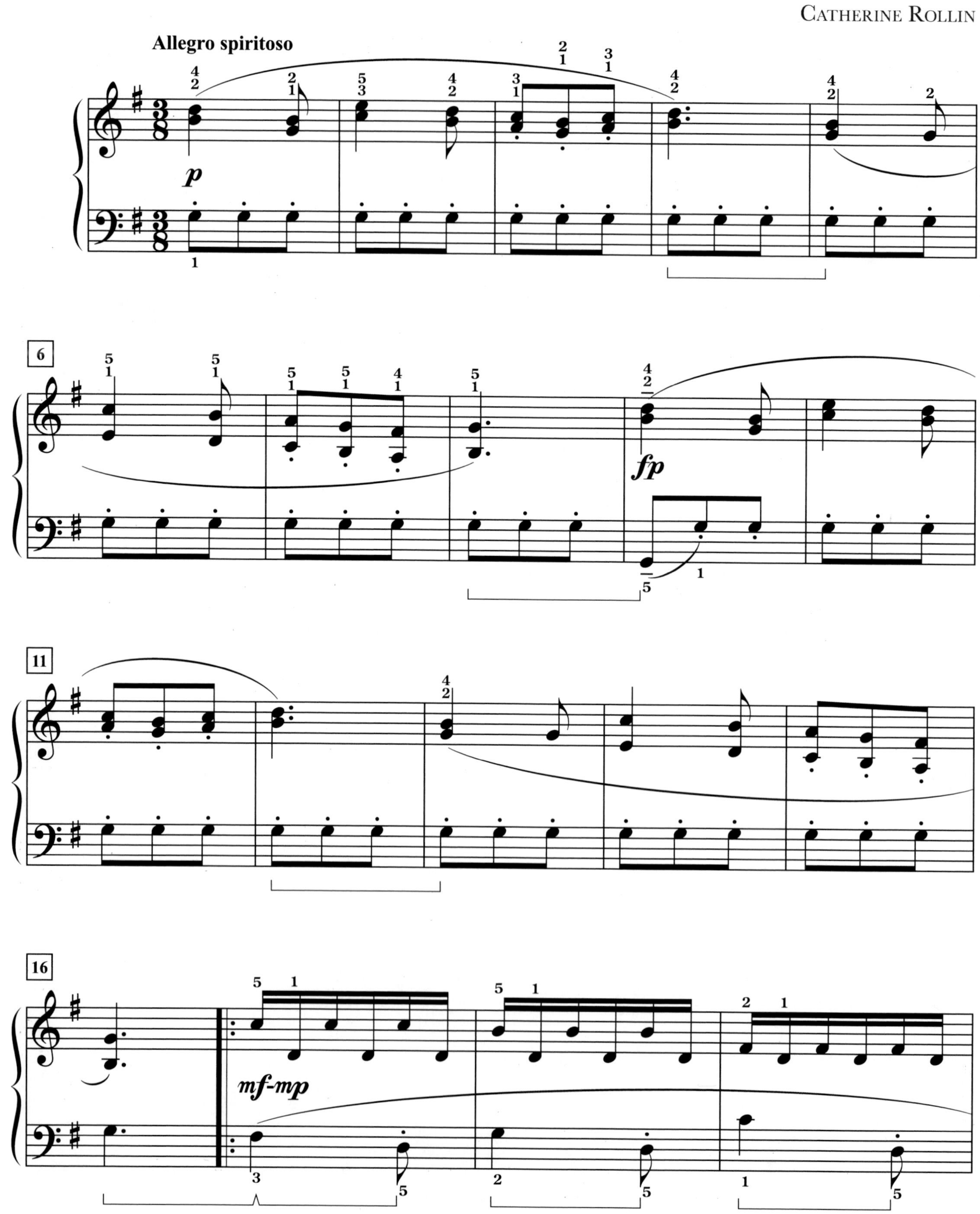

20
cresc.
24
1.
2.
f
f
rit.
29
a tempo
p
34
fp
39

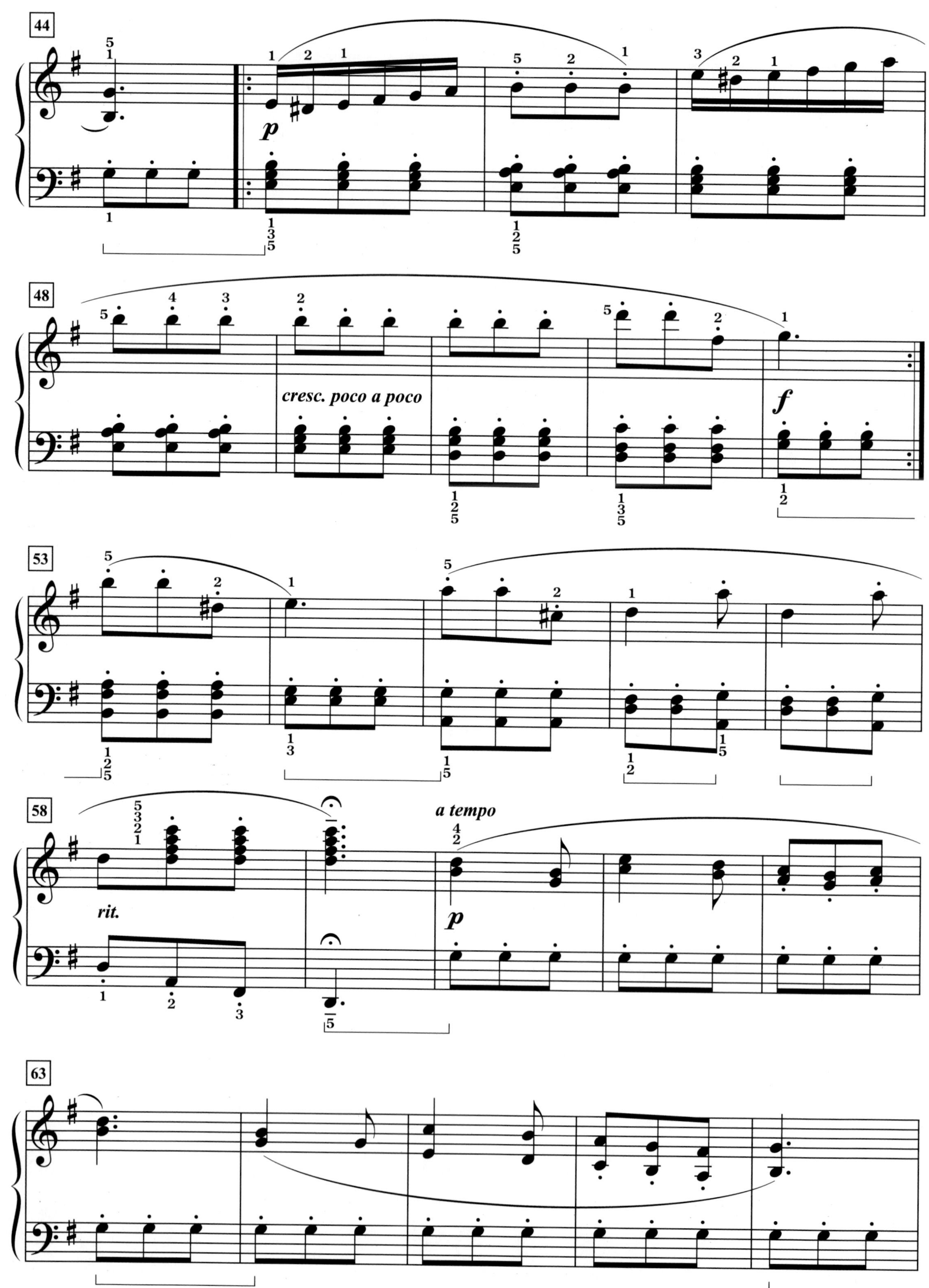
44
p
48
cresc. poco a poco
f
53
58
rit.
a tempo
p
63

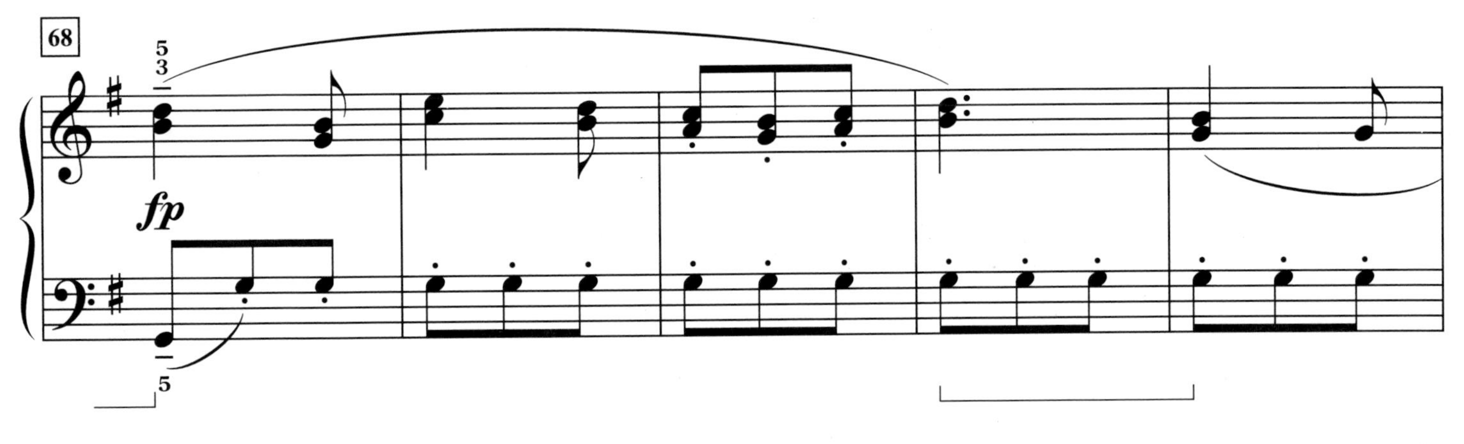
68
fp

73
cresc. poco a poco

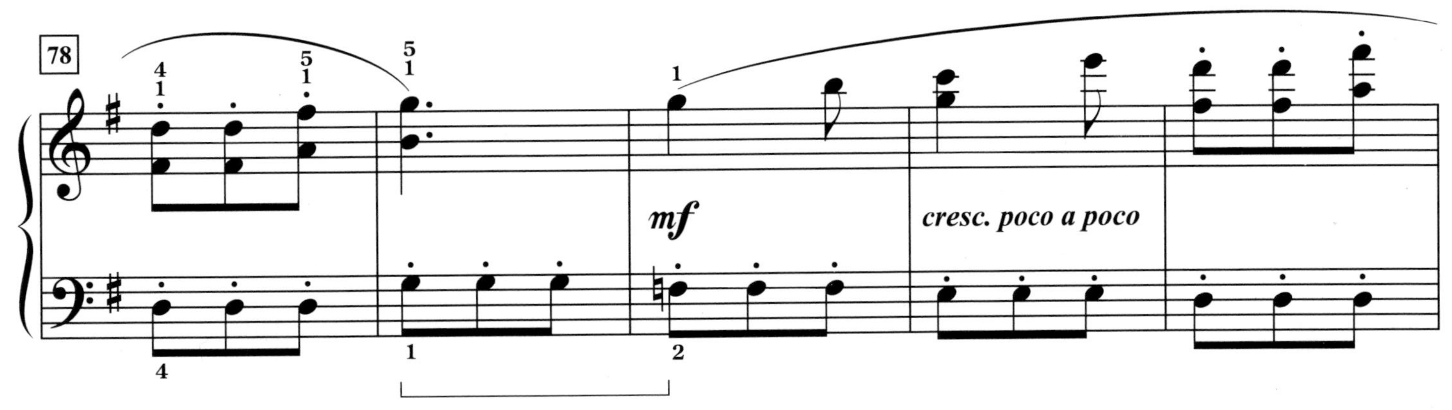
78
mf
cresc. poco a poco

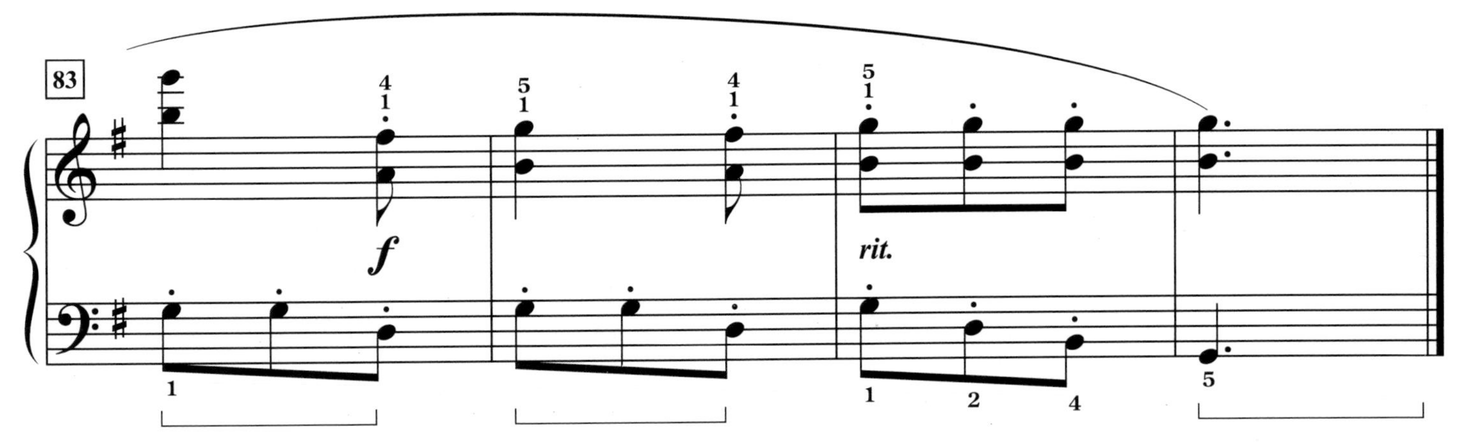
83
f
rit.

Sonatina in C

I.

Catherine Rollin

* Measures 17, 19 and other similar measures should be staccato and not portato.

Classical Style

** In the Classical period, the exposition was traditionally repeated. In this piece, it is the option of the performer.

*** LH portato touch.

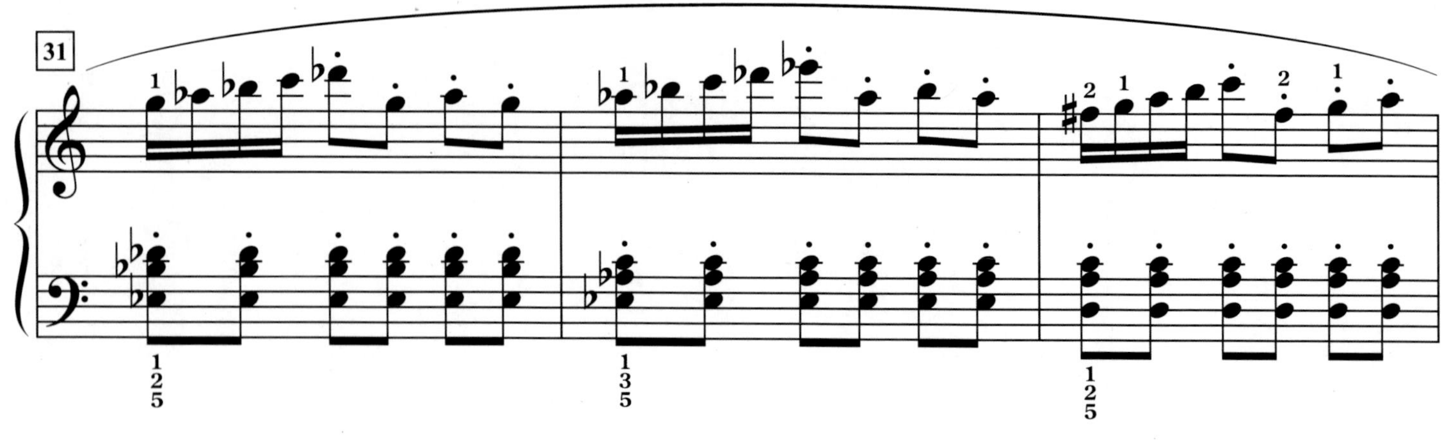
31

34
f
mf

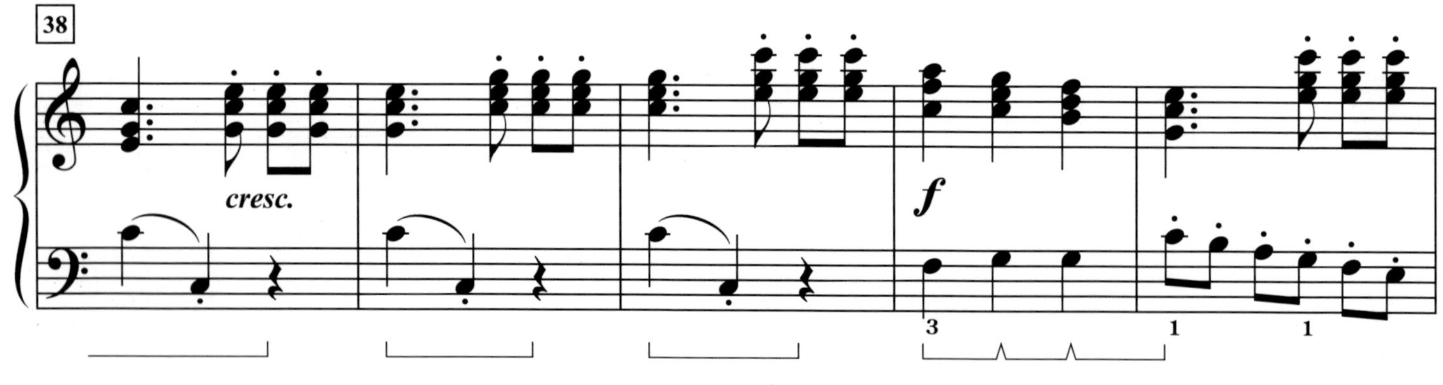
38
cresc.
f

43
mp
cresc.

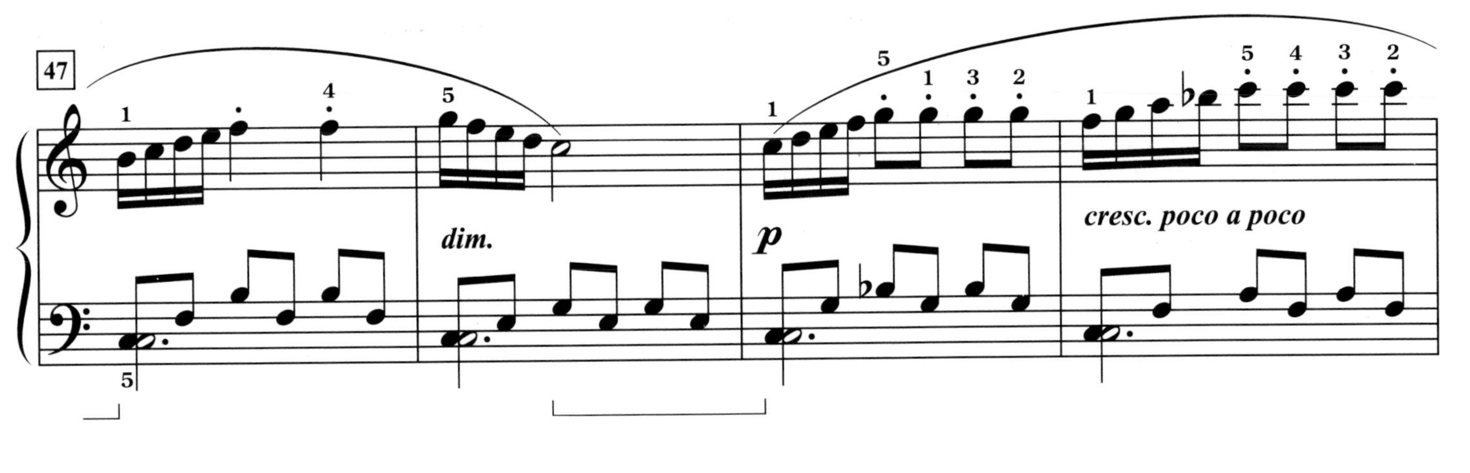
47
dim.
p
cresc. poco a poco

51
f
dim.
mp

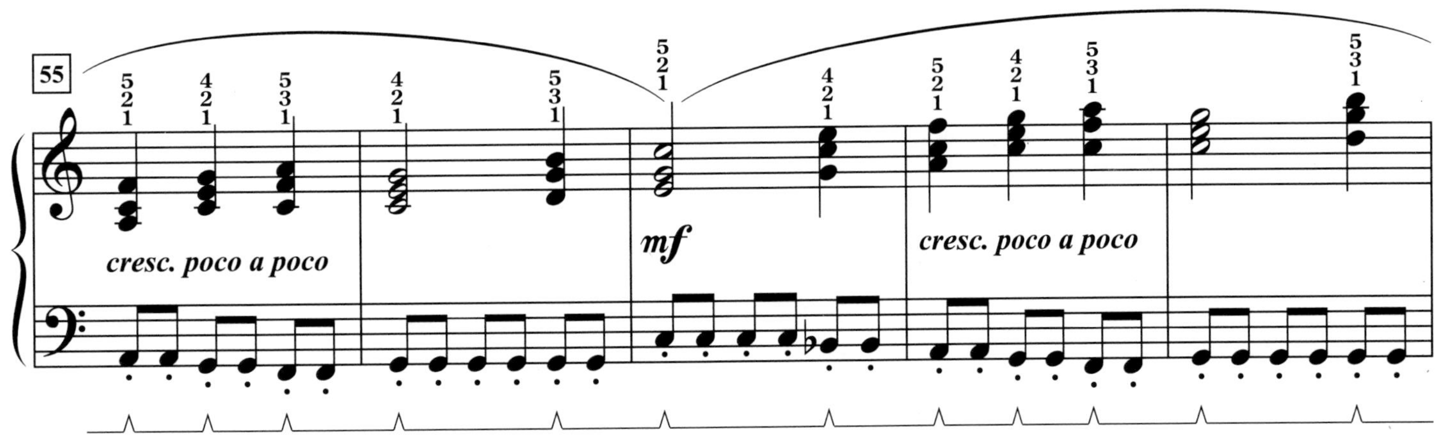
55
cresc. poco a poco
mf
cresc. poco a poco

60
f
rit.

II.

CATHERINE ROLLIN

* It is suggested that finger pedaling be used in the left hand. This is realized as:

13
mp
poco cresc.
mf
poco cresc.

16
a tempo
rit.
pp
poco cresc.
ped. simile

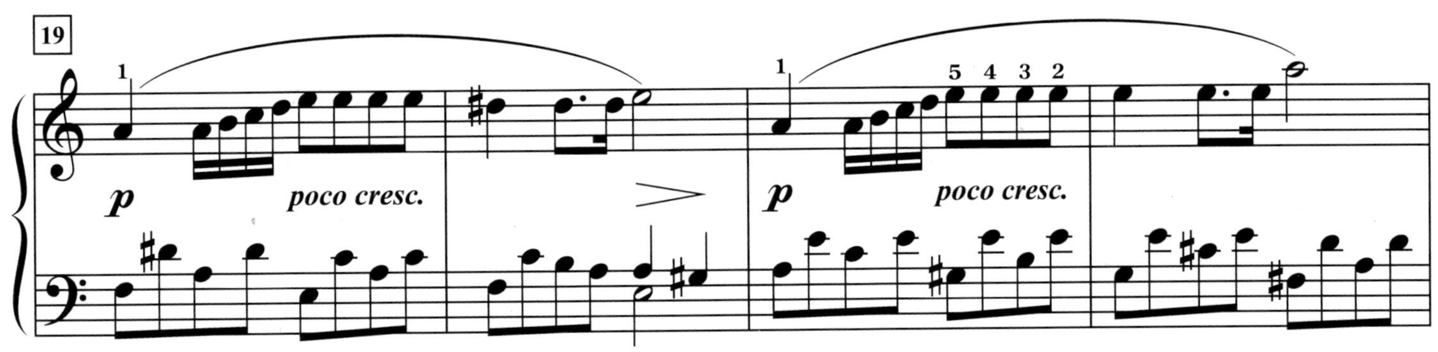
19
p
poco cresc.
p
poco cresc.

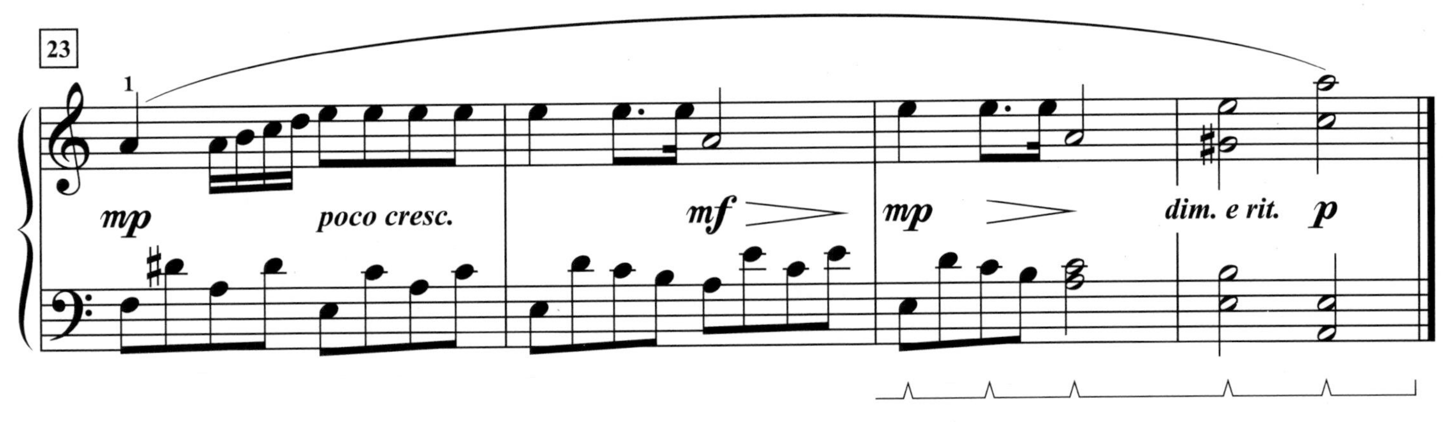
23
mp
poco cresc.
mf
mp
dim. e rit.
p

III.

CATHERINE ROLLIN

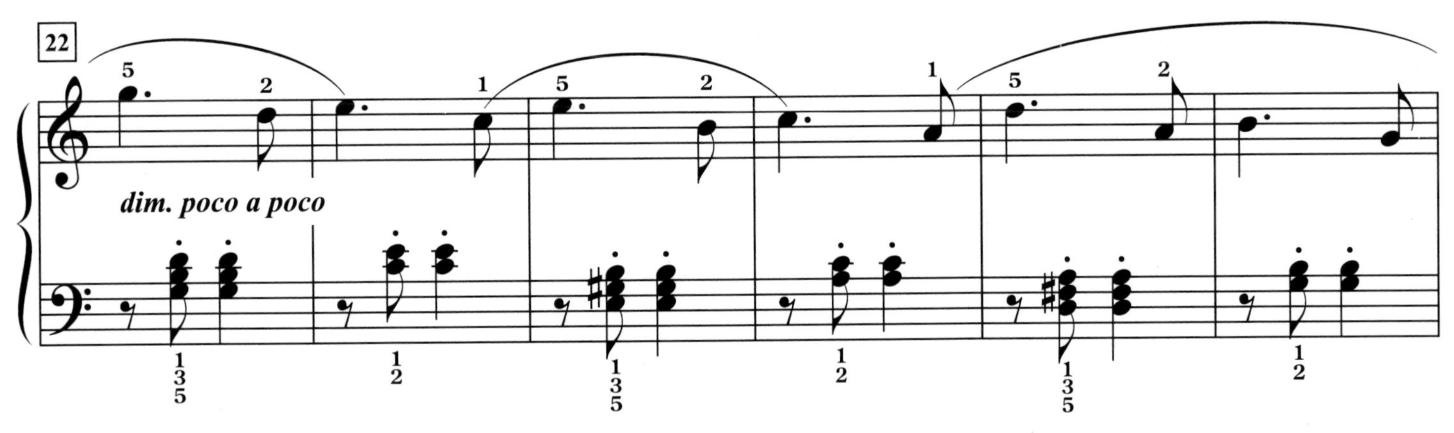
22
dim. poco a poco

28
p
cresc.
rit.

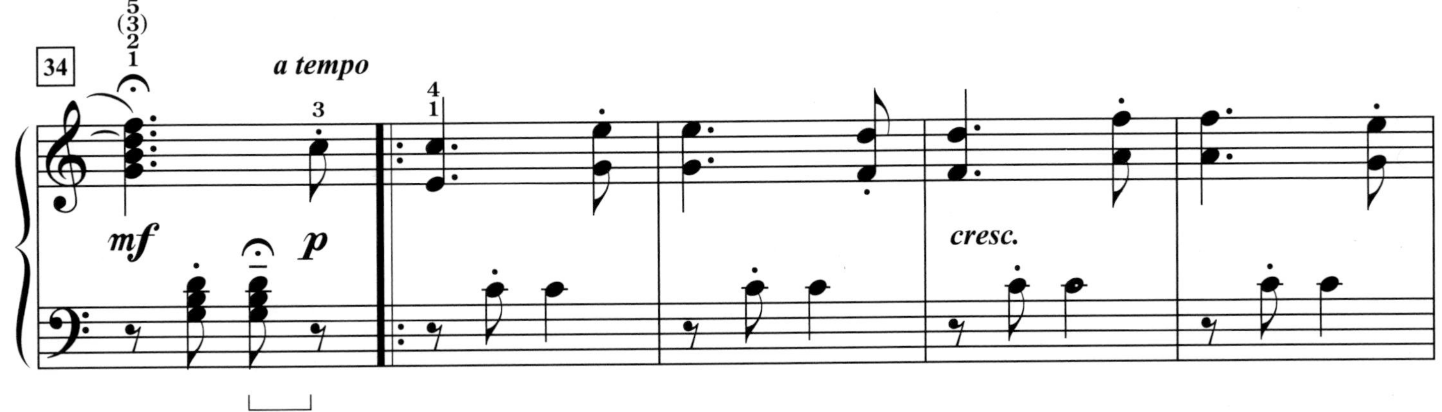
34
a tempo
mf
p
cresc.

39
1.
2.
mf
dim.
p

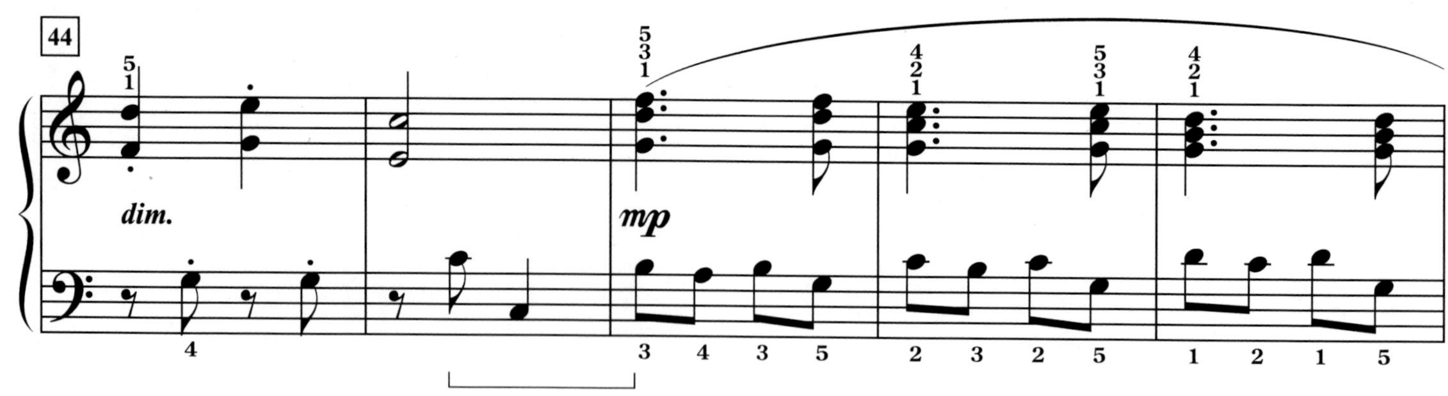
44
dim.
mp

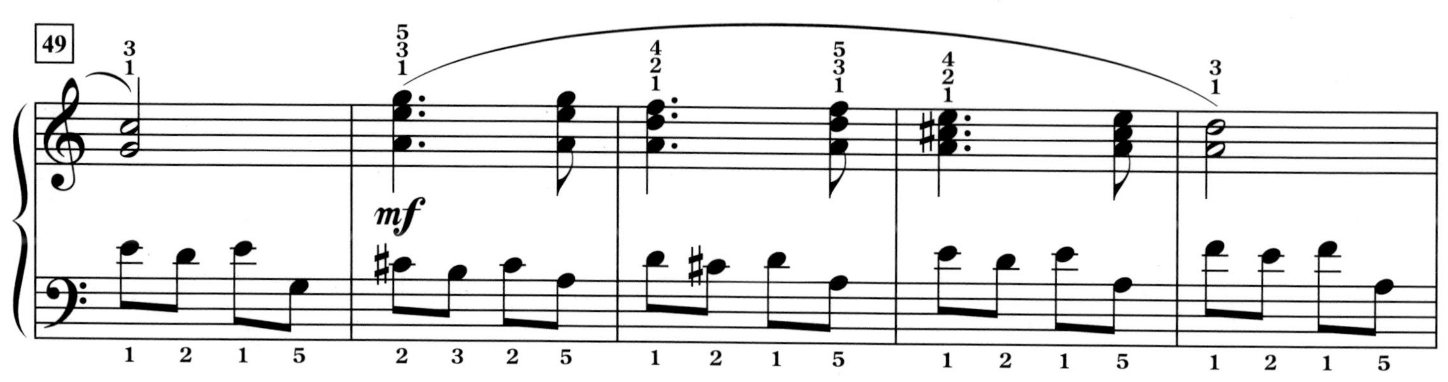
49
mf

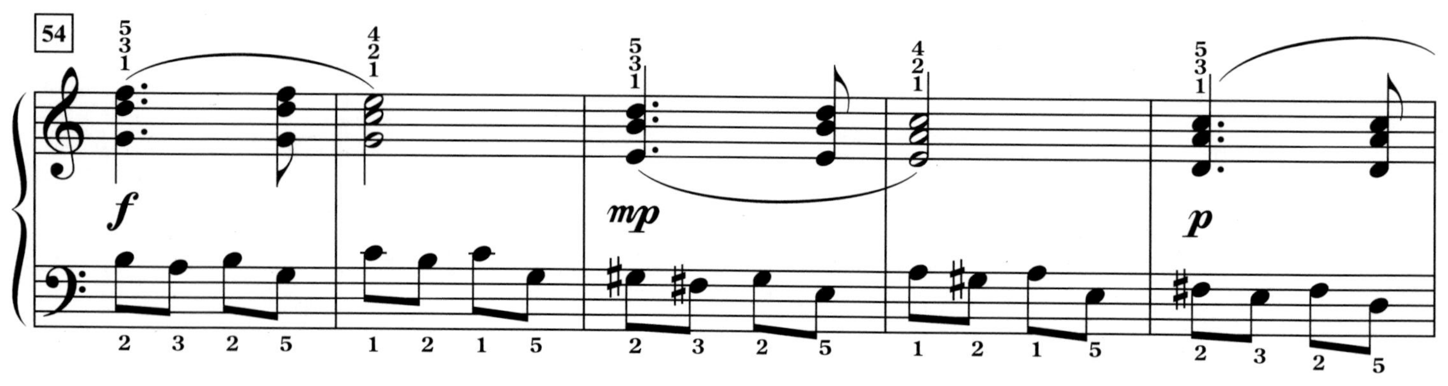
54
f
mp
p

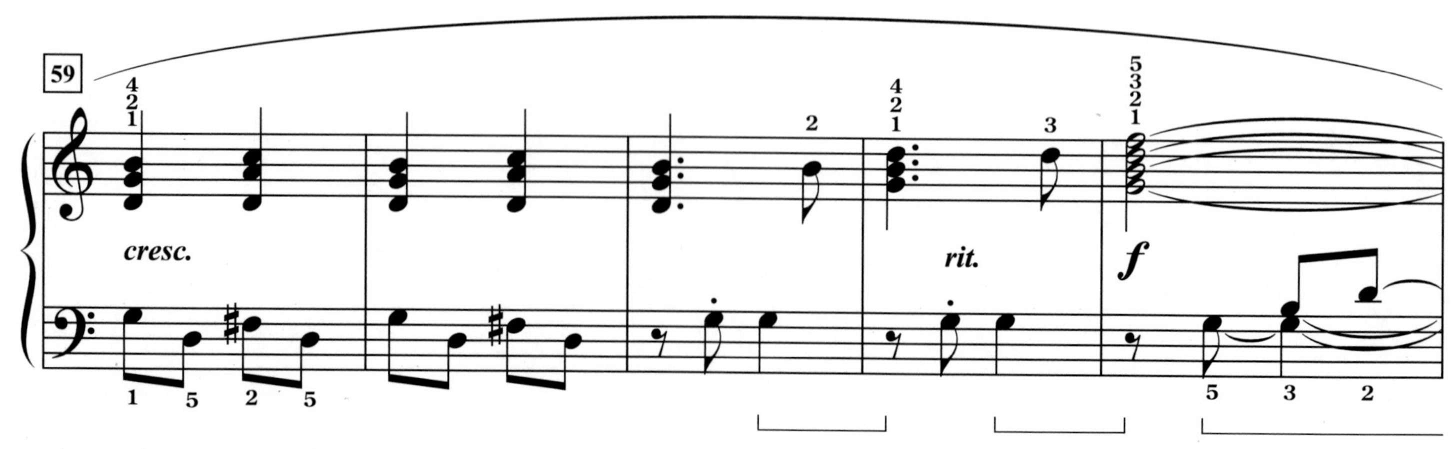
59
cresc.
rit.
f

64
a tempo
mf
(p on repeat)
1

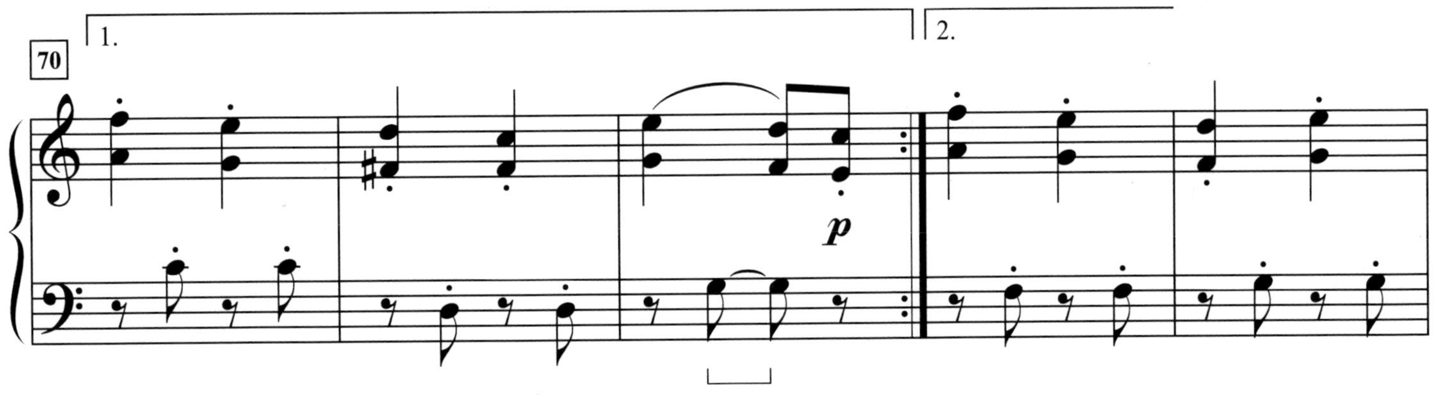
70
1.
2.
p

75
5
3
1
5
2
1
4
2
1
p cresc.
mf
cresc. poco a poco
1

81
f rit.
1
1
1
2
4
5

Variations on an Original Theme*

Catherine Rollin

THEME

* Although it is intended for this piece to be performed in its entirety, it is an option to play selected variations only.

18
mp
22
Variation I
L'istesso tempo
p
26
1.
2.
poco cresc.
mp
31
mf
mp
cresc.
35
f
f

39
a tempo
dim. e rit.
44
poco cresc.
Variation 2
Poco piú mosso
poco rit.
49
triplets cont.
53
triplets cont.
57
cresc.

61
cresc.
cresc.
65
a tempo
poco rit.
69
Variation 3
Tempo primo
molto legato
74
simile
80
a tempo
poco rit.
cresc.

86
cresc.
91
a tempo
p
mp
poco rit.
96
Variation 4
Piú vivace
p
mp
poco rit.
101
104
1.
2.
mf
mp

107
cresc.
mp
cresc.
110
mp
cresc.
113
f
116
a tempo
poco rit.
mp
119

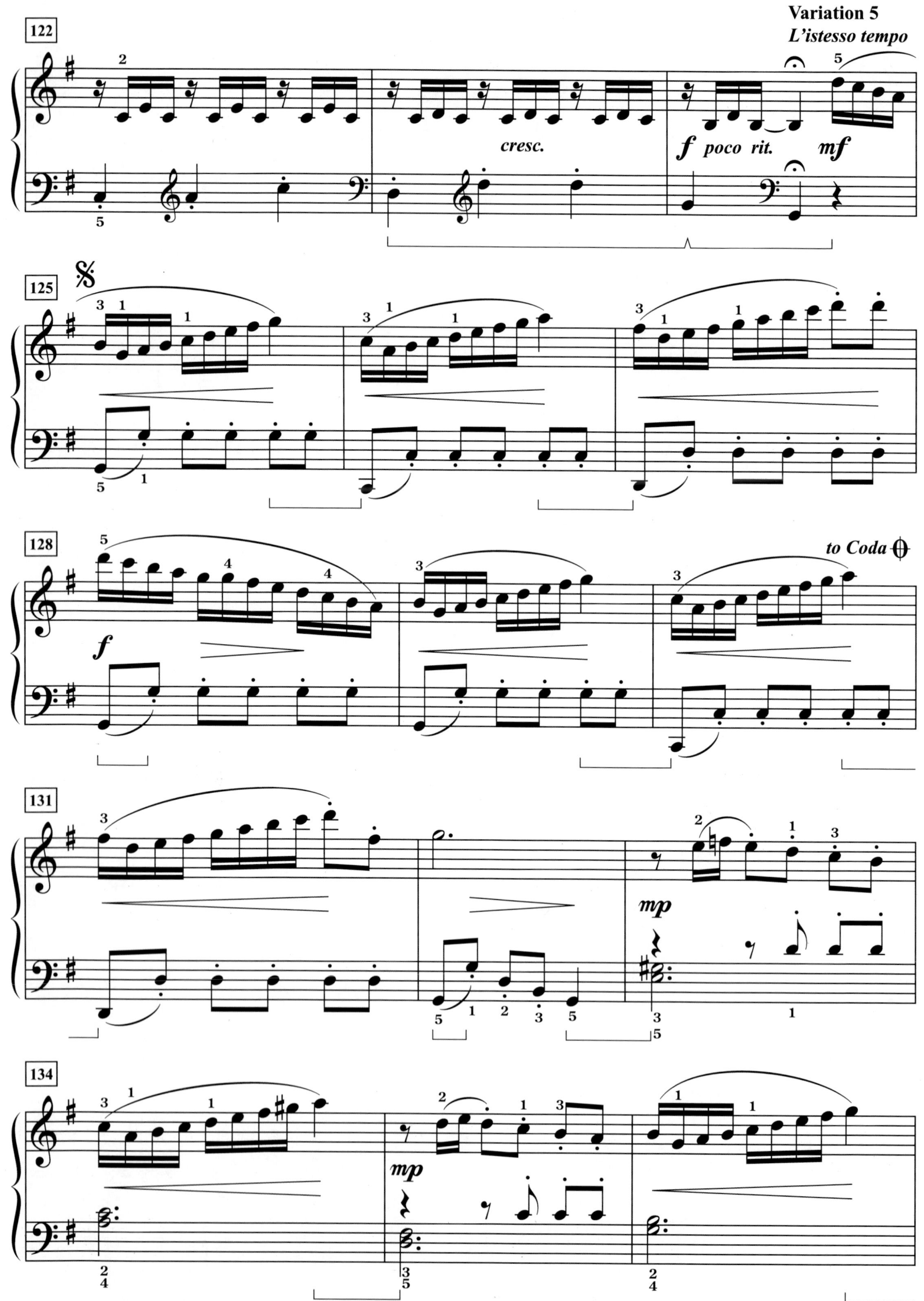
122
Variation 5
L'istesso tempo
cresc.
f poco rit.
mf
125
128
f
to Coda
131
mp
134
mp

137
p
dim. e poco rit.

140
a tempo
cresc.
f

143
D.S. al Coda
mf
Coda
rit.
a tempo
mp
molto cresc.

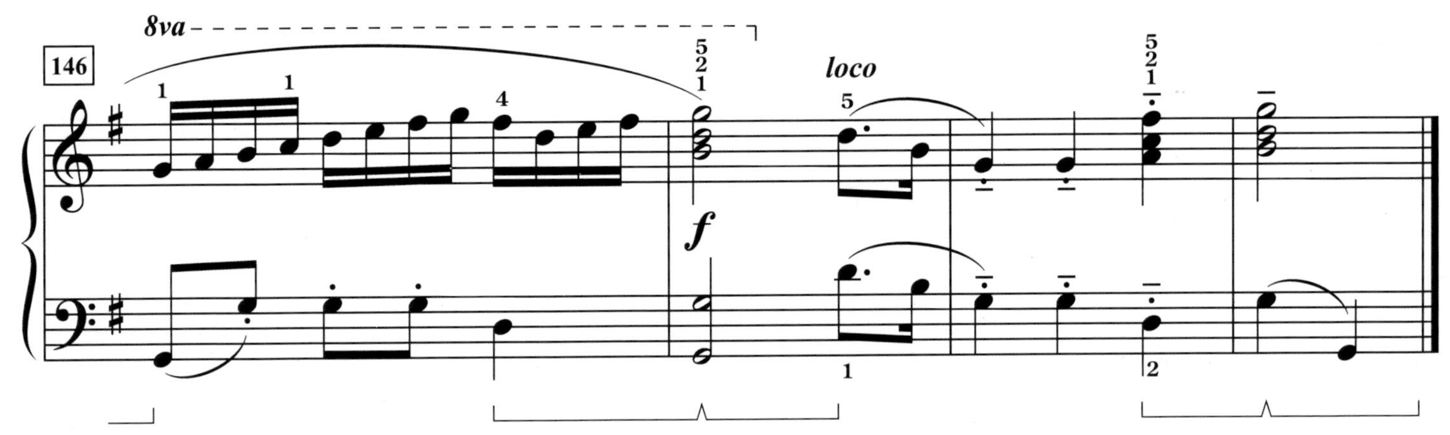
146
8va
f
loco

Classic Minuet

Catherine Rollin

17
p
mp
22
a tempo
rit.
mf
27
32
p
37
rit.

Nocturne

Catherine Rollin

13
mp
cresc.
dim.

16
a tempo – poco più mosso
poco rit.
mp

19
mf
cresc.

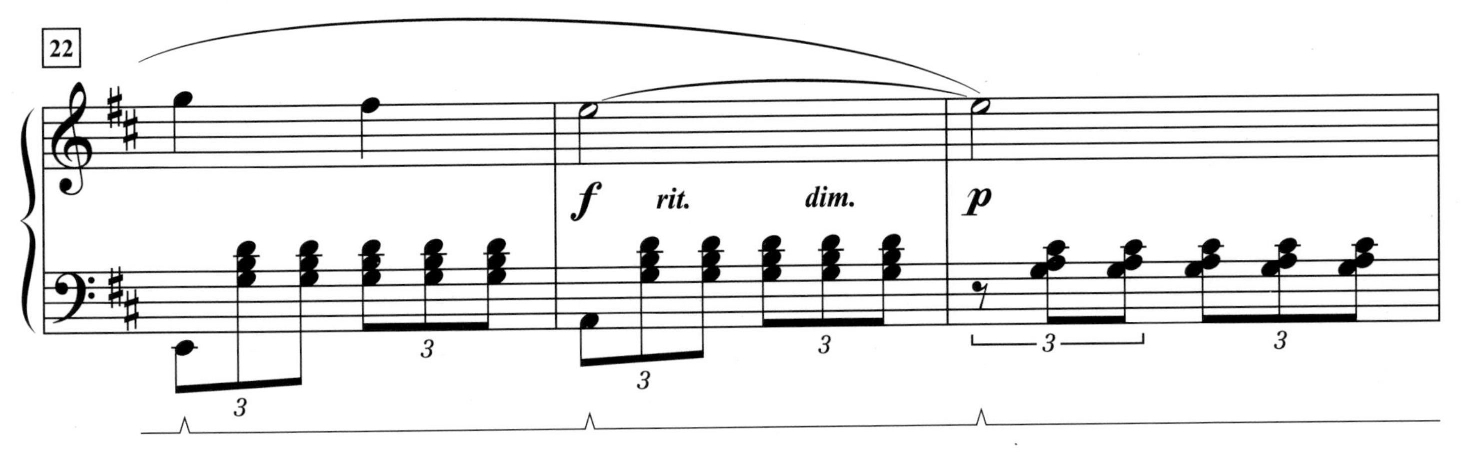
22
f
rit.
dim.
p

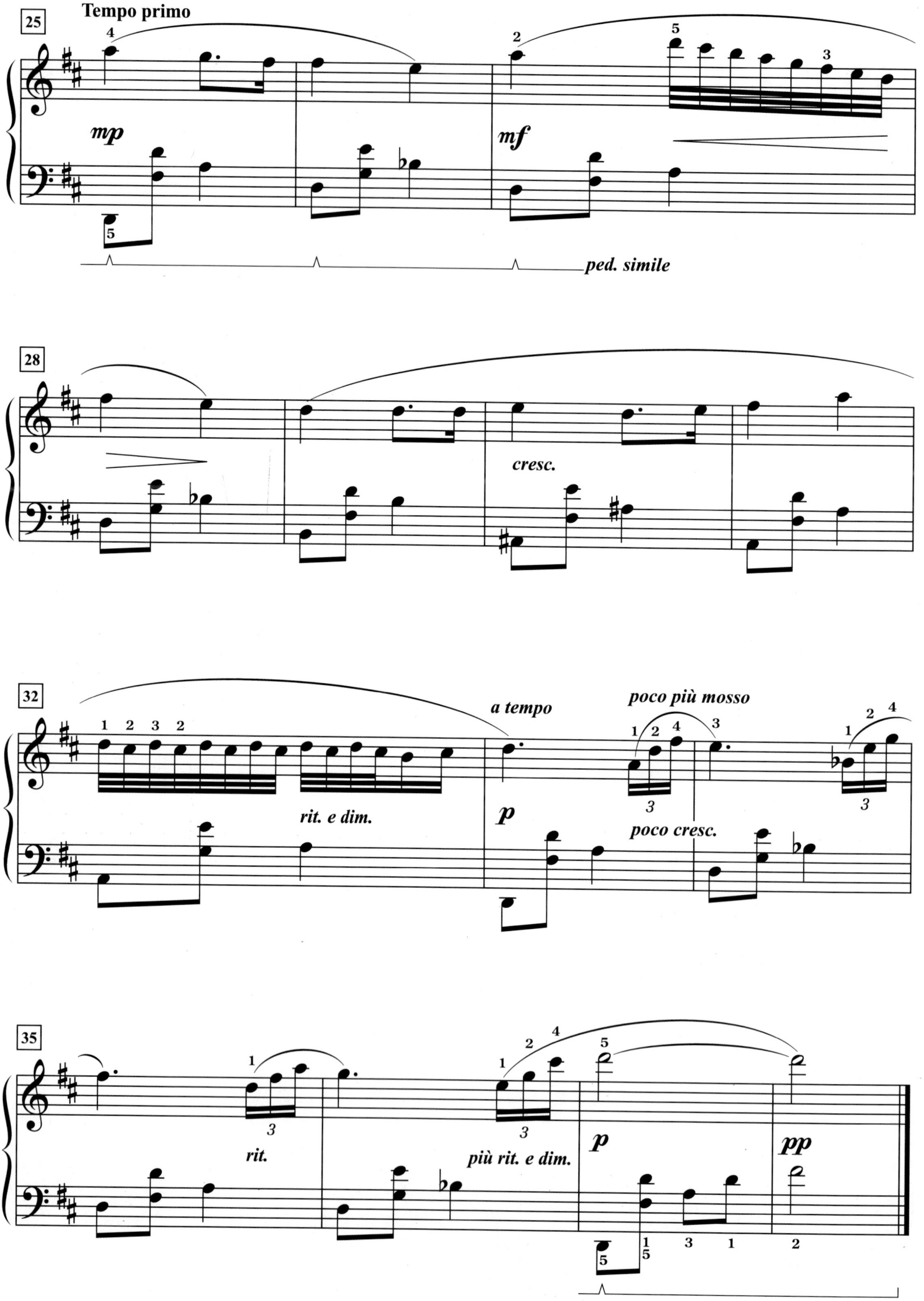
25
Tempo primo
mp
mf
ped. simile
28
cresc.
32
a tempo
poco più mosso
rit. e dim.
p
poco cresc.
35
rit.
più rit. e dim.
p
pp

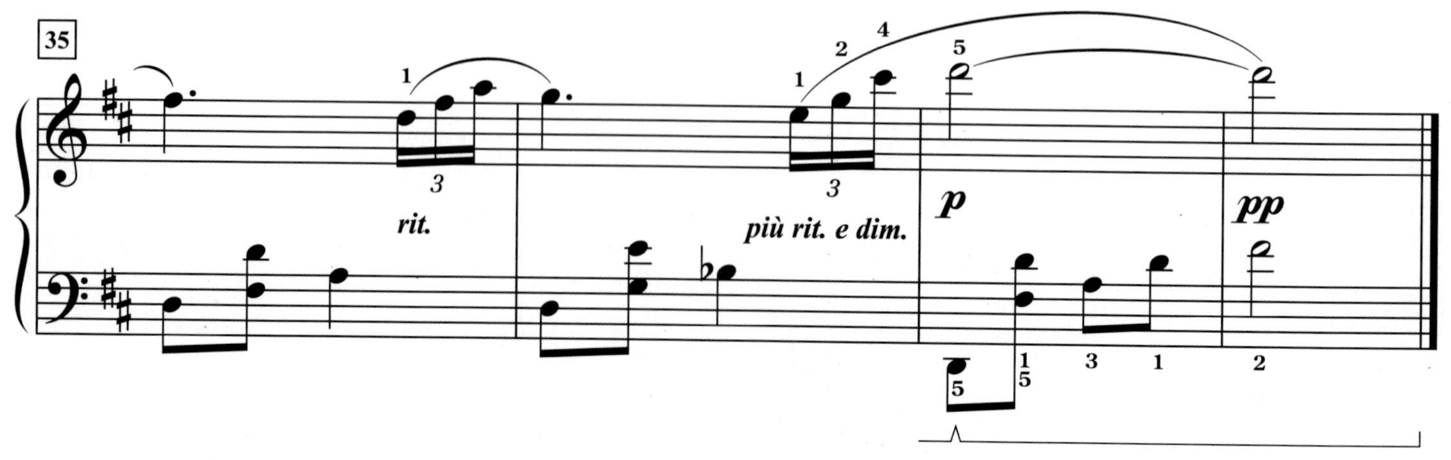

MAZURKA

CATHERINE ROLLIN

Romantic Style

17
mp
mf
20
mp
23
mf
26
cresc.
f
dim. e molto rit.
p

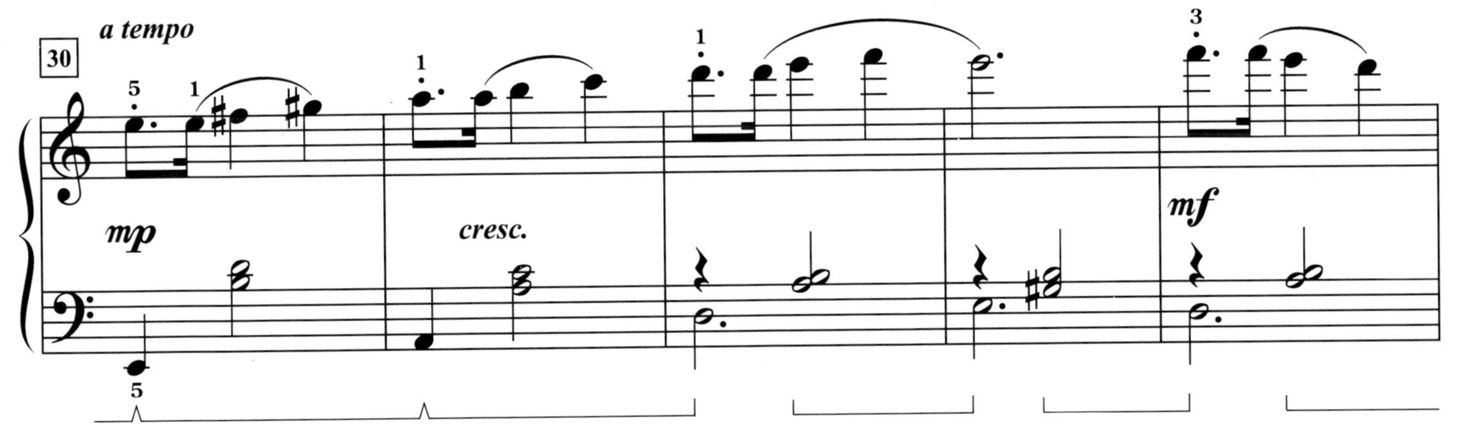
30
a tempo
mp
cresc.
mf

35
dim.
p
cresc.

40
mp
dim.
p rit.

45
a tempo
mp
poco rit.
p

Waltz

Catherine Rollin

19
mf
24
p
poco rit.
più vivace
mp-mf
28
ped. simile
32
Molto vivace
1.
2.
cresc. poco a poco
37
8va
poco rit.
f

Etude

Catherine Rollin

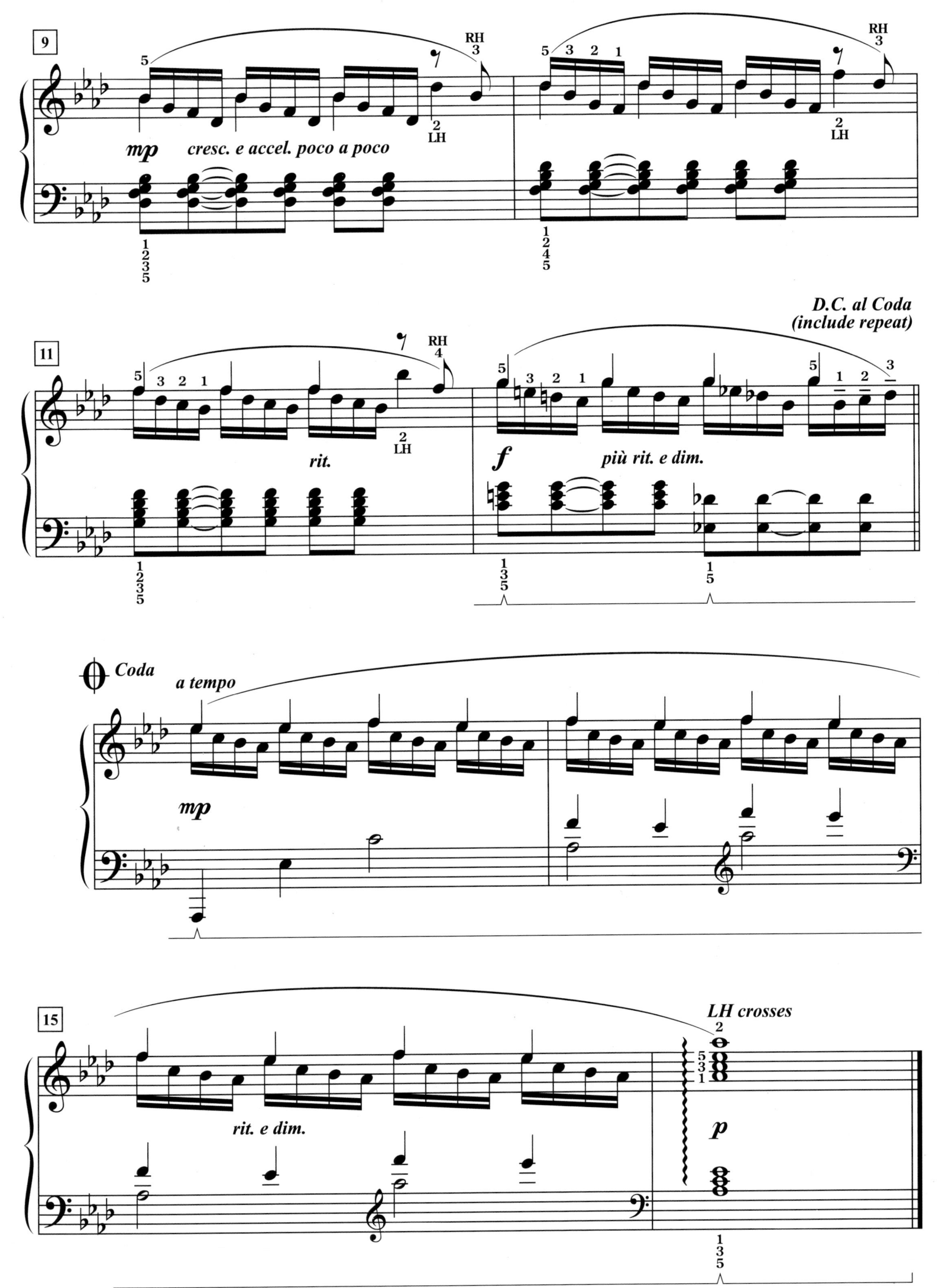

Romantic Style

Polonaise

Catherine Rollin

13
mf
f

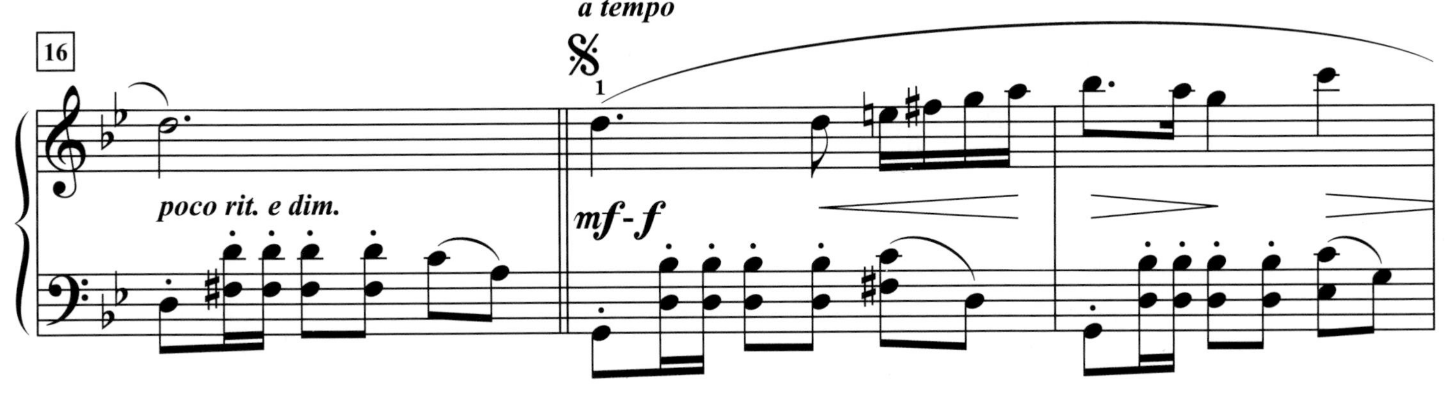
16
a tempo
poco rit. e dim.
mf-f

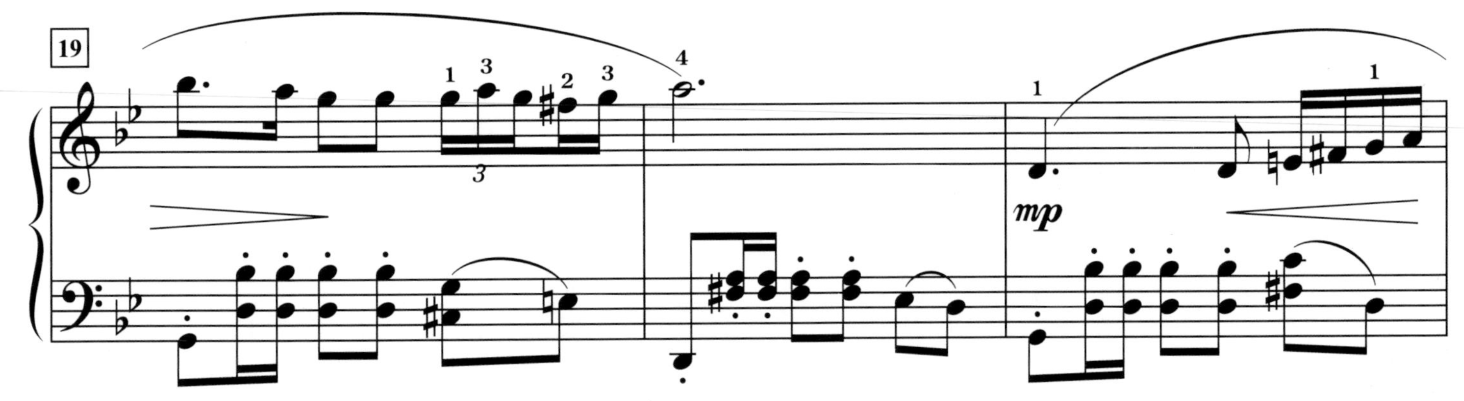
19
mp

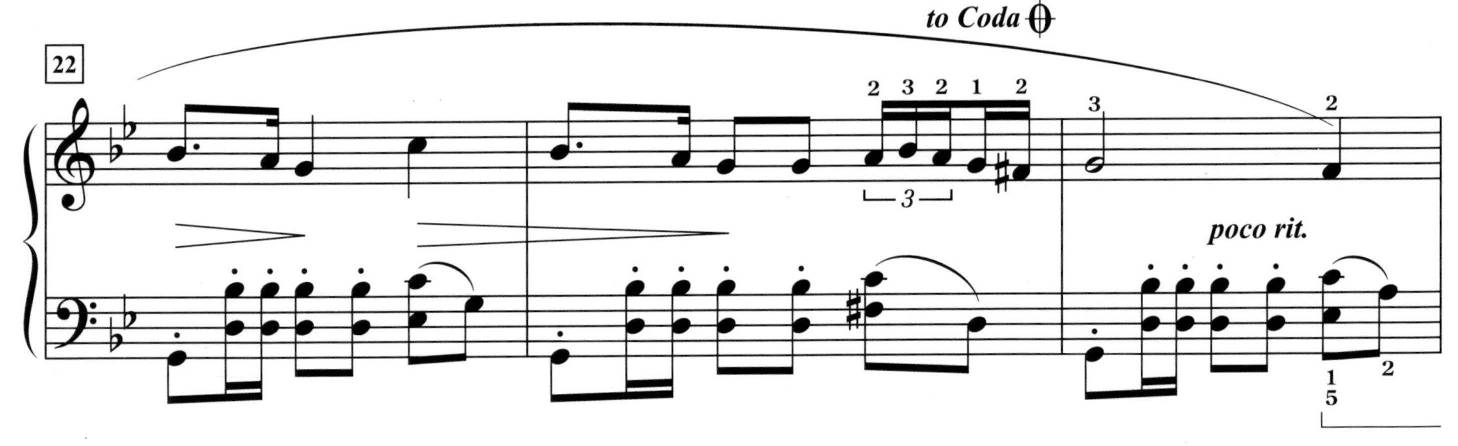
22
to Coda
poco rit.

a tempo
p
mp
mf
f
D.S. al Coda
mf
rit.
cresc.
Coda
p
mp
dim. e rit.
p

FOR VERA ROLLIN BURKE

CHOUCHOU'S CAKEWALK

CATHERINE ROLLIN

Impressionist Style

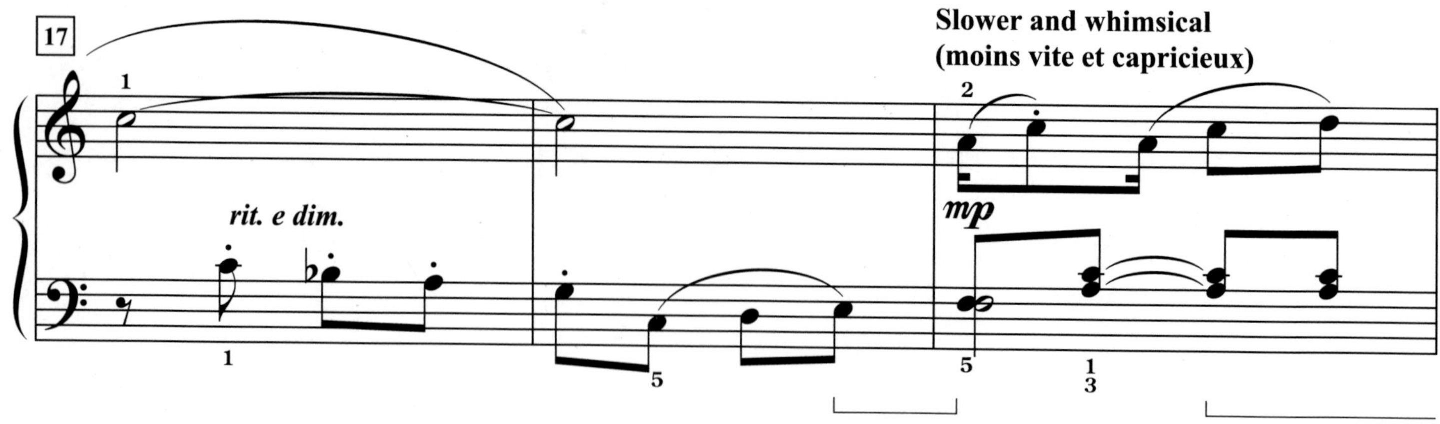
17
Slower and whimsical
(moins vite et capricieux)
rit. e dim.
mp

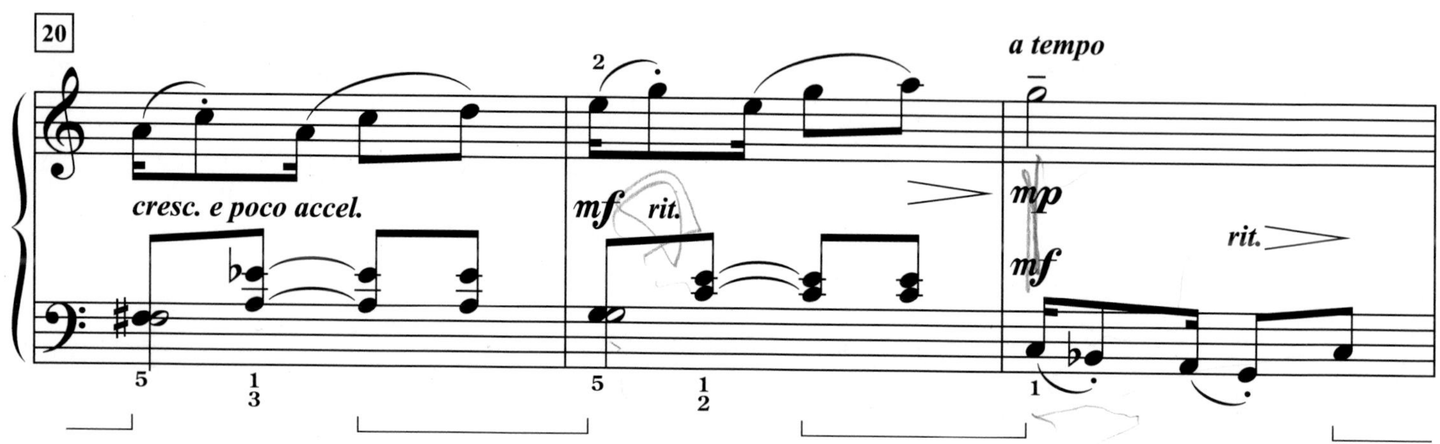
20
a tempo
cresc. e poco accel.
mf
rit.
mp
mf
rit.

23
a tempo
mp
cresc. e poco accel.
mf
rit.

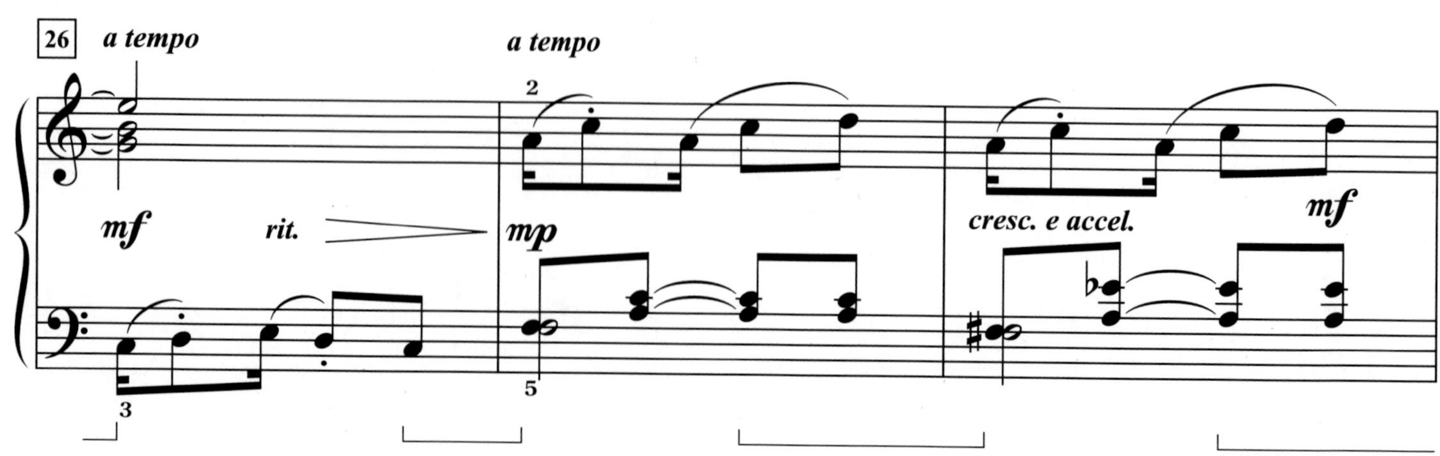
26
a tempo
a tempo
mf
rit.
mp
cresc. e accel.
mf

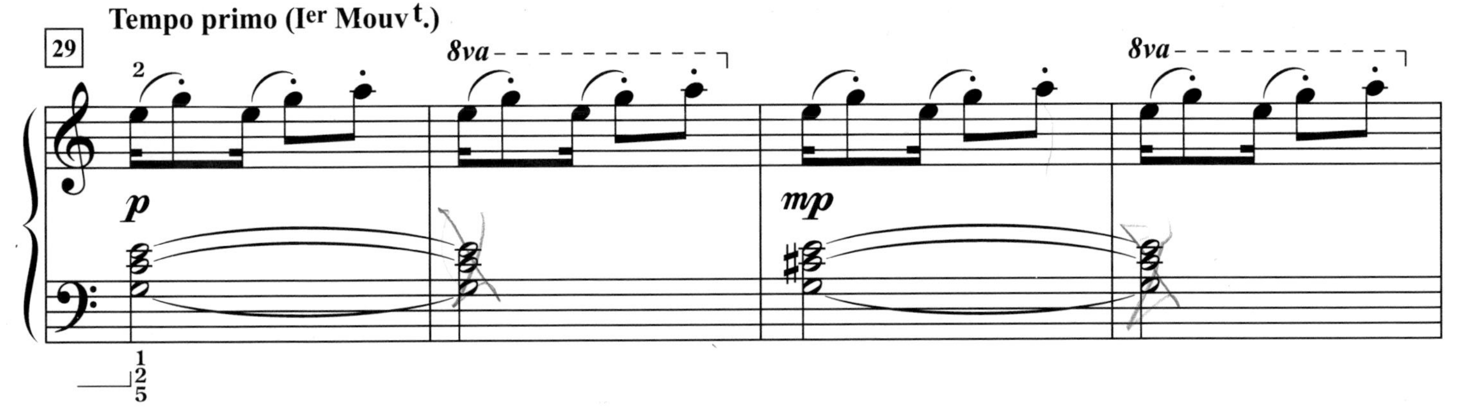
29
Tempo primo (Ier Mouvt.)
8va
8va
p
mp

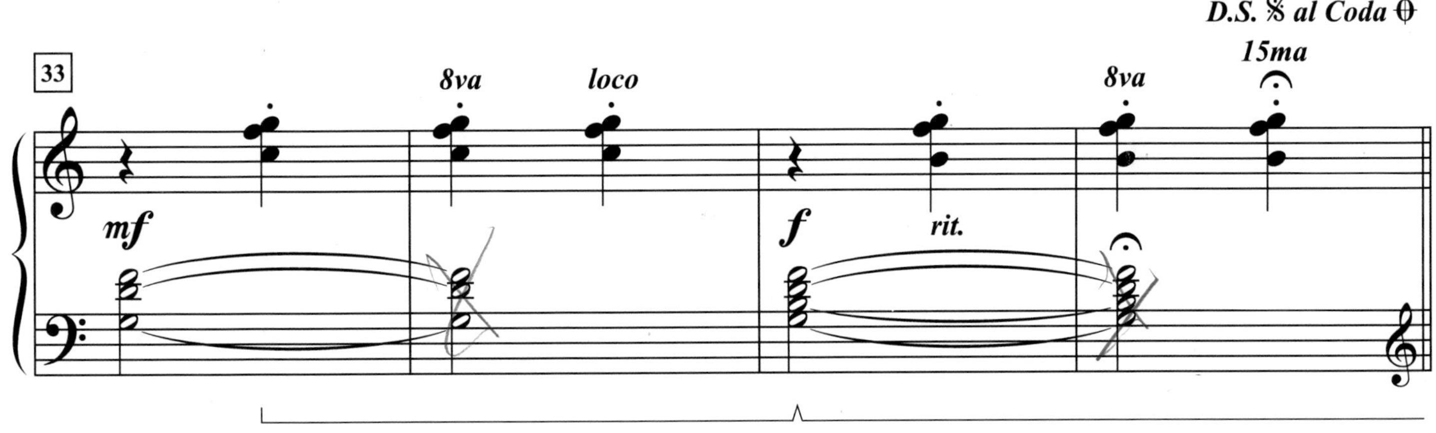
33
D.S. 𝄋 al Coda 𝄌
8va
loco
8va
15ma
mf
f
rit.

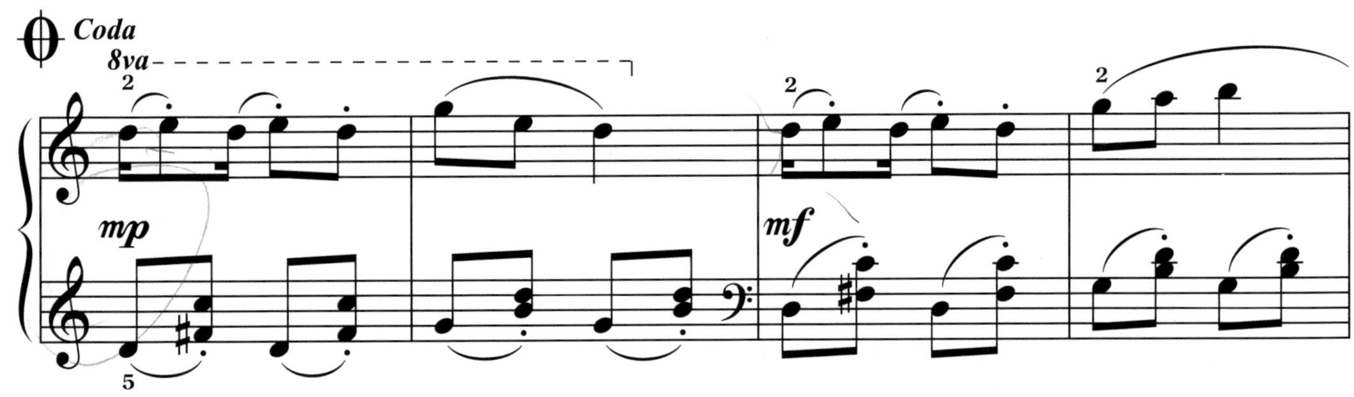
Coda
8va
mp
mf

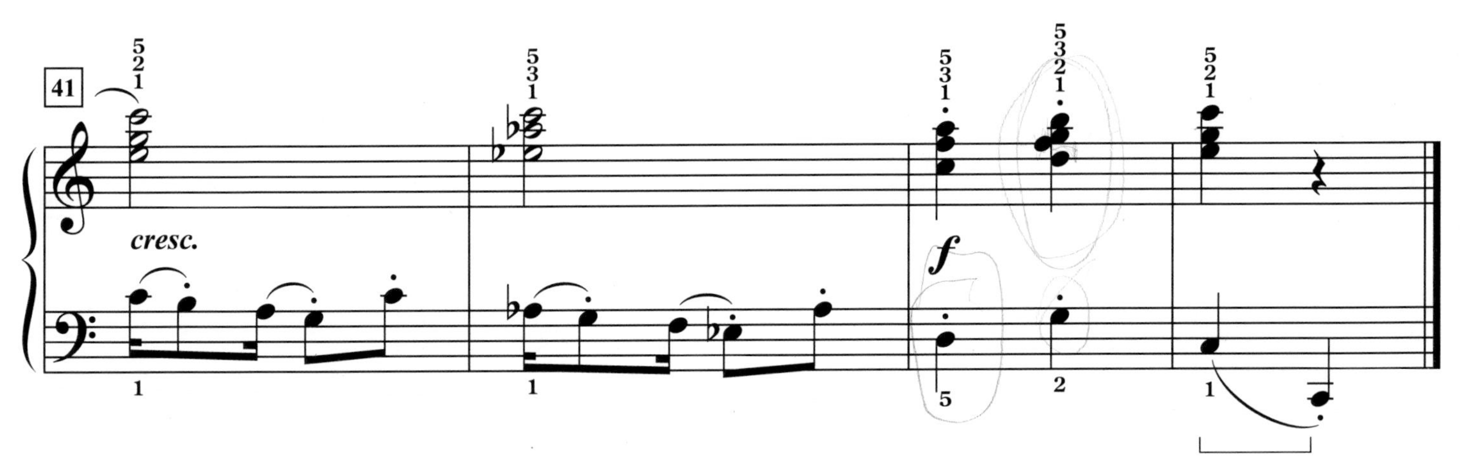
41
cresc.
f

Under the Sea
(Sous la mer)

Catherine Rollin

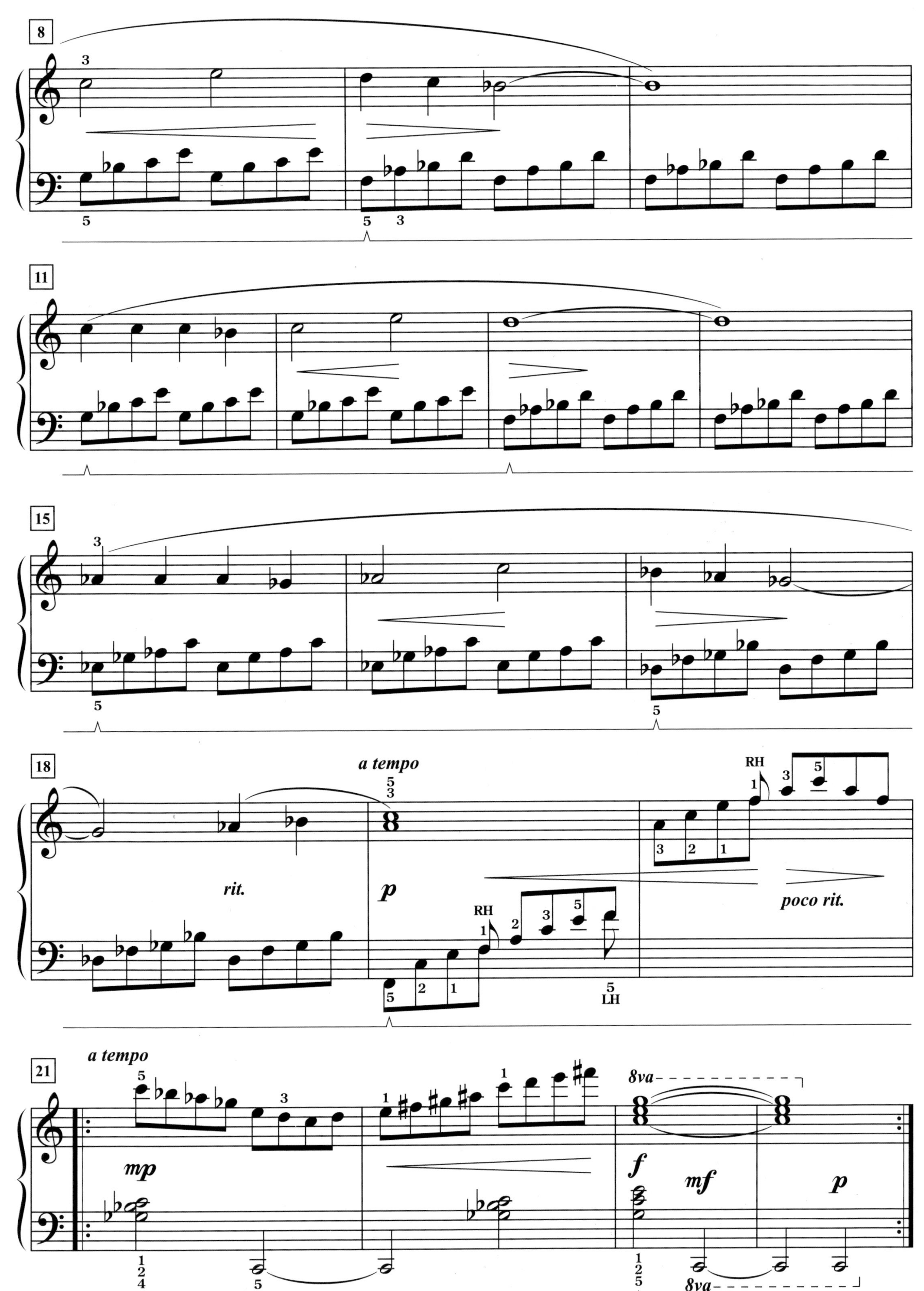

Impressionist Style

* Bring out and play the LH 5th finger cantabile.

*Hold back slightly then accelerando little by little to measure 43, where the tempo should be almost twice as fast as the starting tempo at measure 41.

FOR ALLEGRA LILLY

IBERIA

CATHERINE ROLLIN

Impressionist Style

42
expressive (expressif)
dim.
pp
mf
47
1.
f
p
52
2.
Boldly
D.C. al Coda
f
rit.
Coda
mf
59
a tempo
molto rit.
f
RH
LH
8va

Windchimes
(Carillons dans le vent)

Catherine Rollin

Impressionist Style

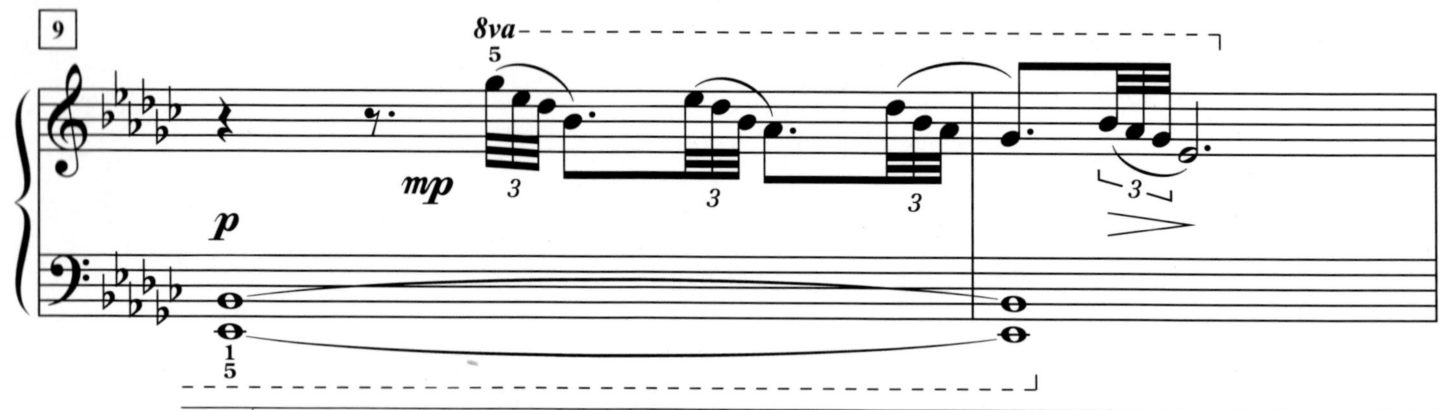

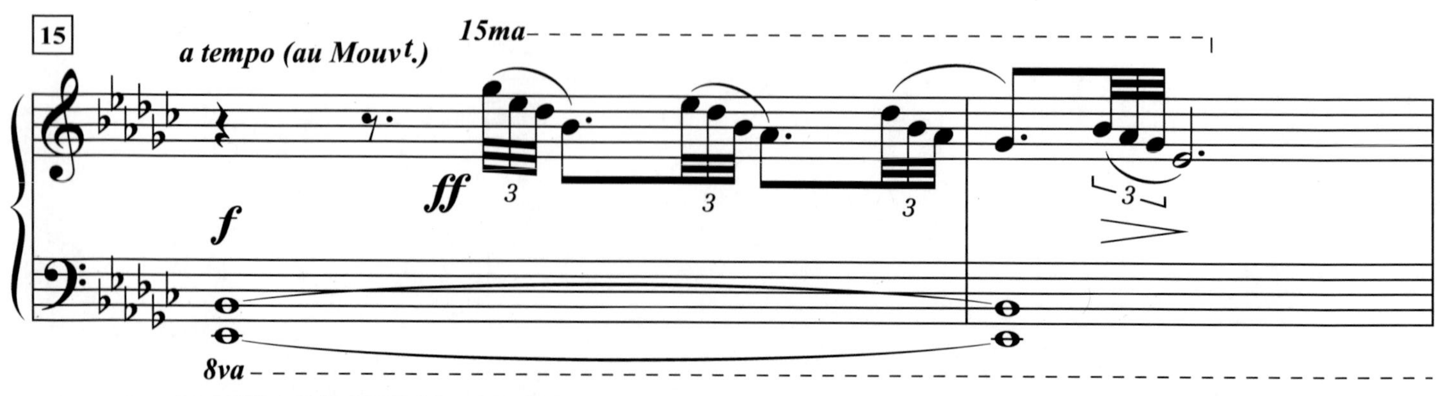

* Hold back slightly and reach "a tempo" by beat 3.

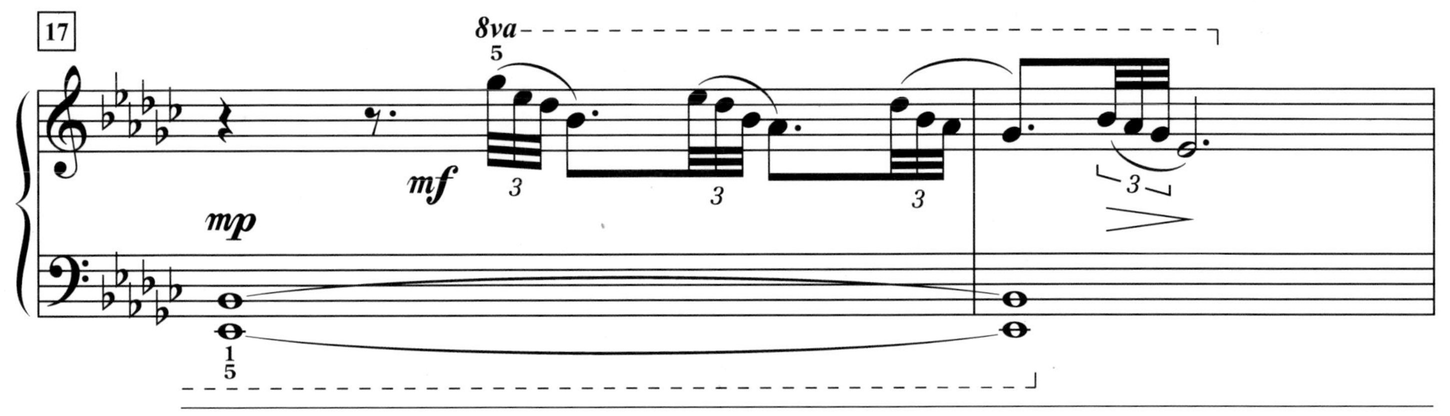
17
8va
5
mf
mp
3
3
3
3
1
5

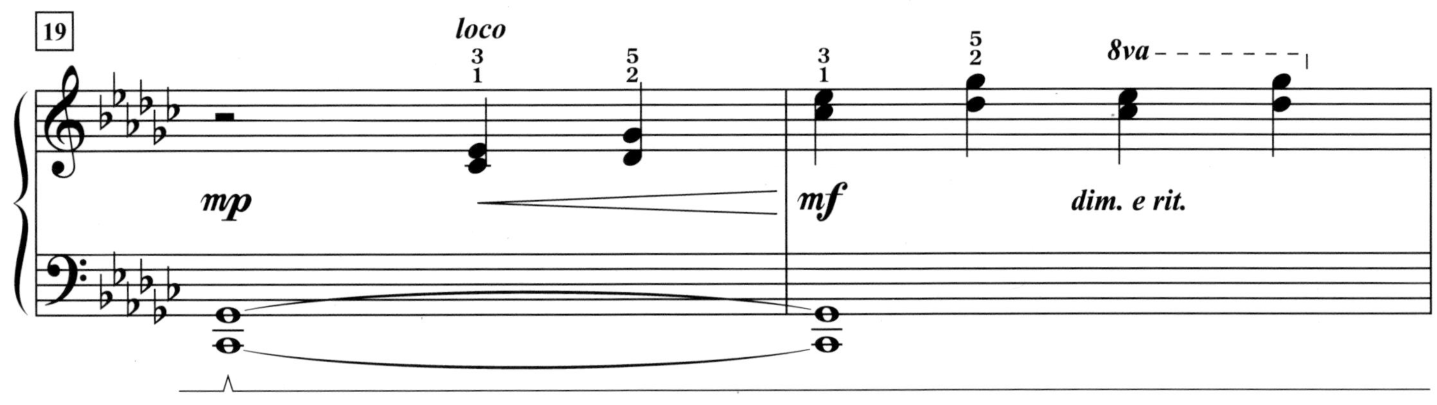
19
loco
3
1
5
2
3
1
5
2
8va
mp
mf
dim. e rit.

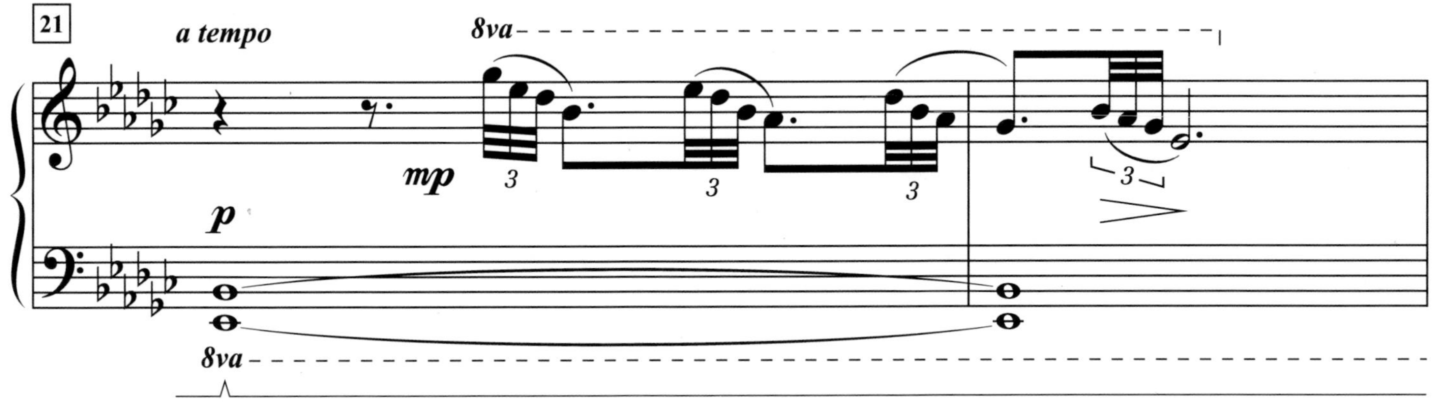
21
a tempo
8va
mp
p
3
3
3
3
8va

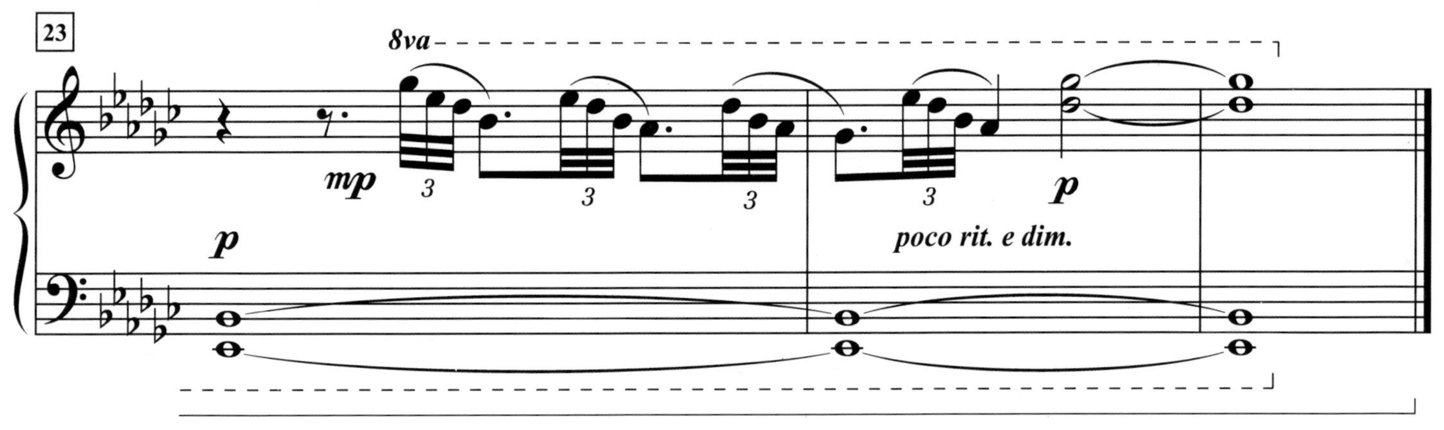
23
8va
mp
p
3
3
3
3
p
poco rit. e dim.

Water Lilies
(Nénuphars)

Catherine Rollin

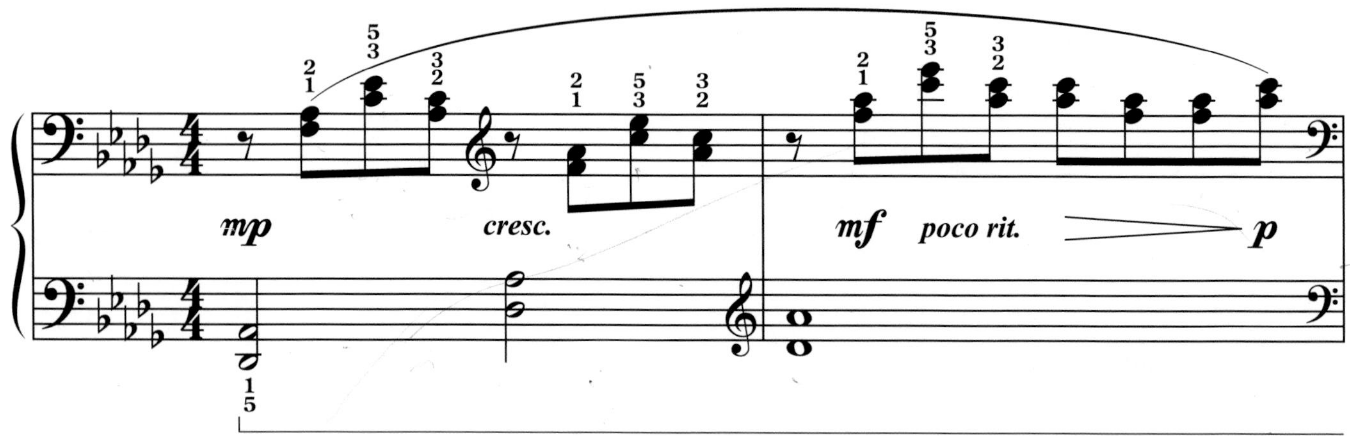

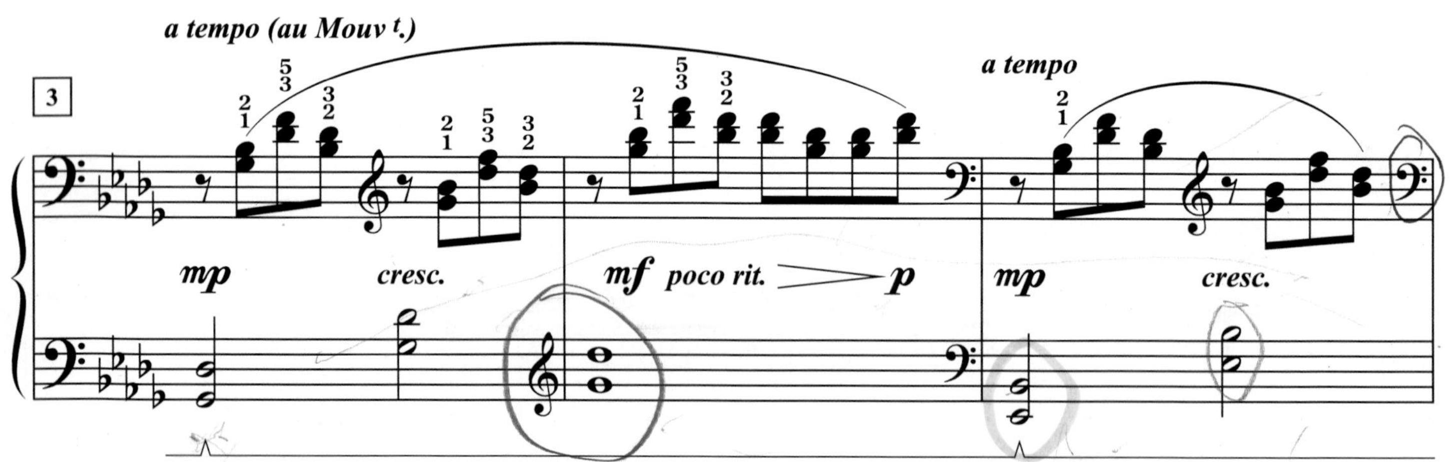

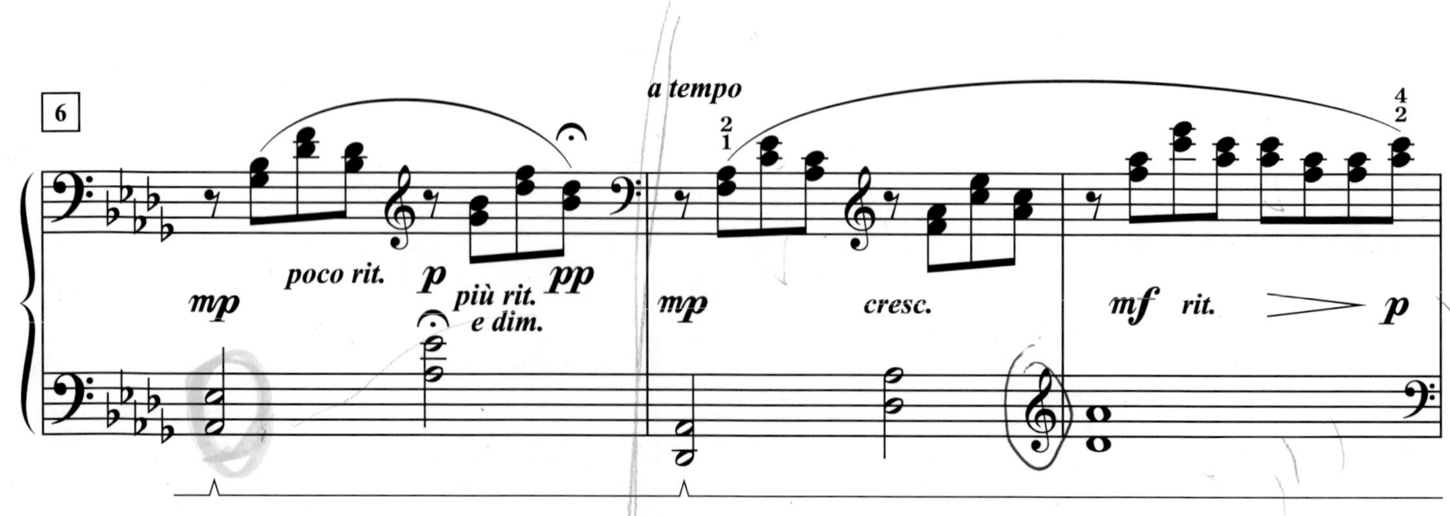

9
a tempo
a tempo
RH
LH
mp
poco rit.
mf
dim.
p
poco rit.
11
a tempo
a tempo
mp
poco rit.
mf
dim.
p
poco rit.
13
a tempo
mf
f
dim.
p
poco rit.
15
a tempo
mf
rit.
dim.
p

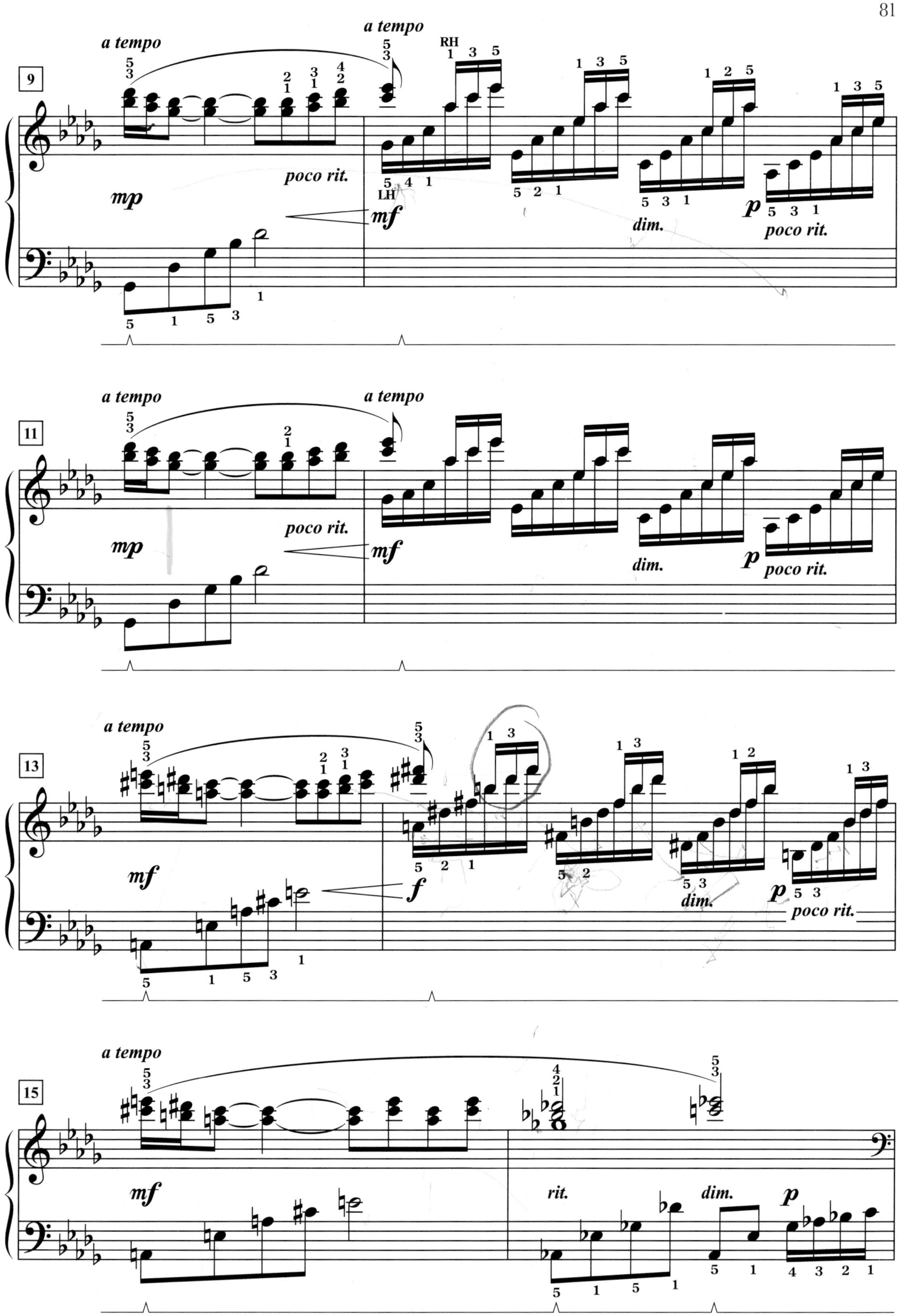

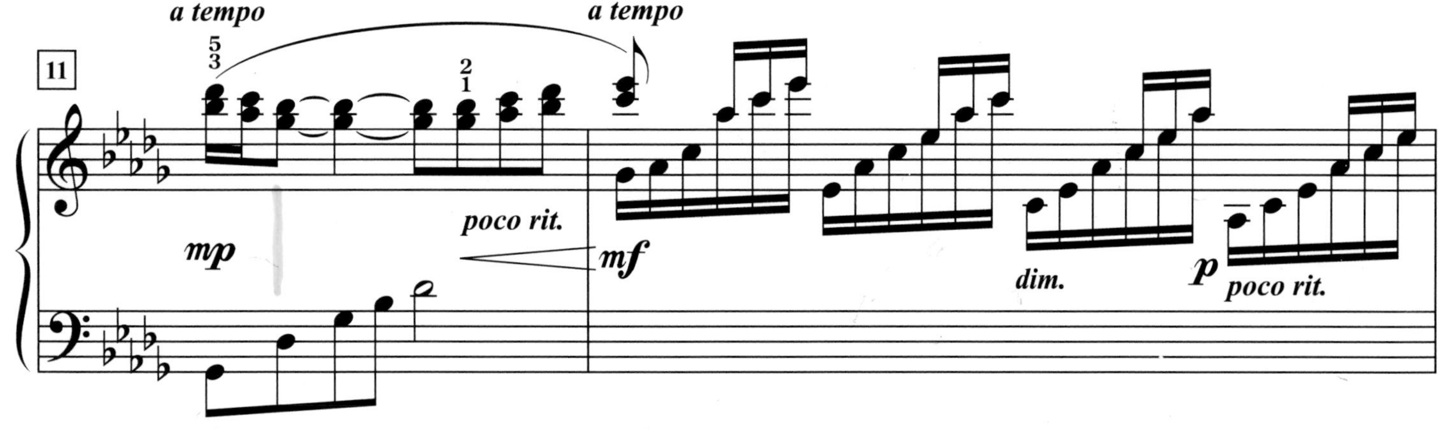

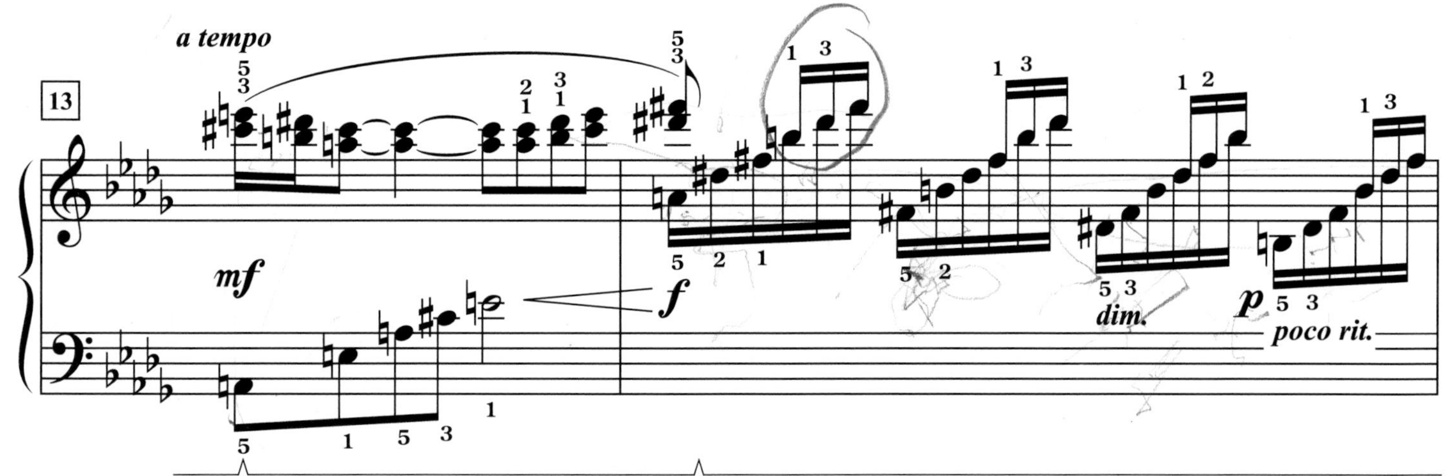

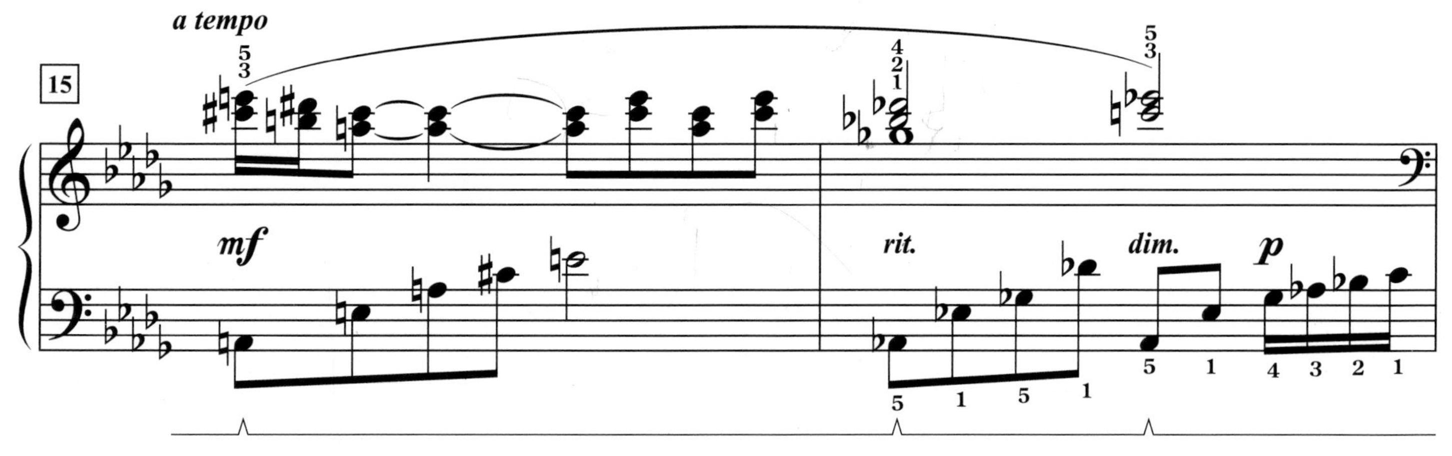

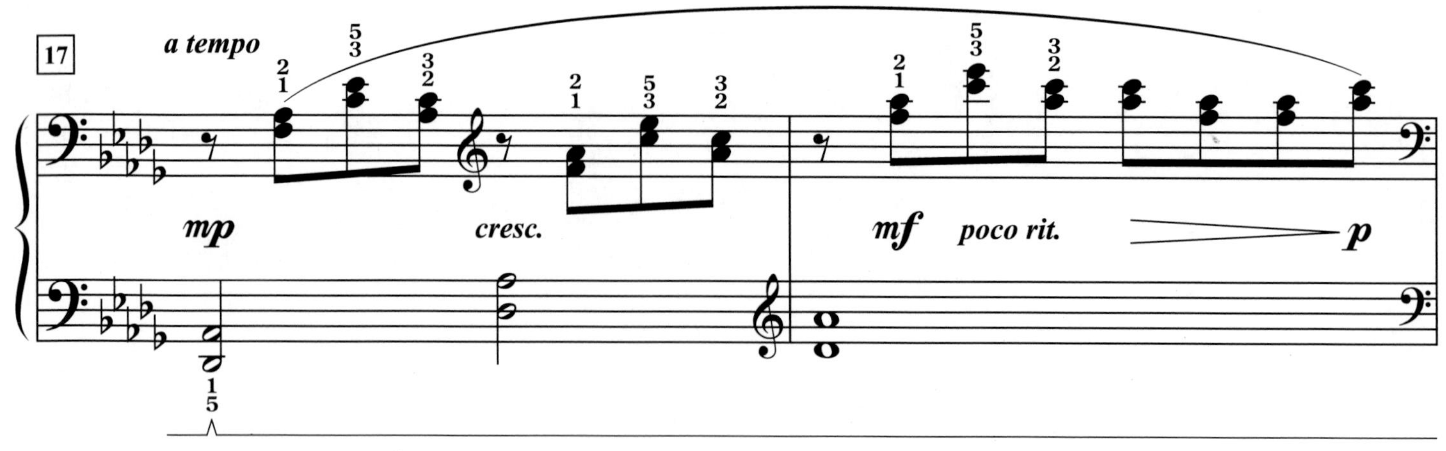
17
a tempo
mp
cresc.
mf
poco rit.
p

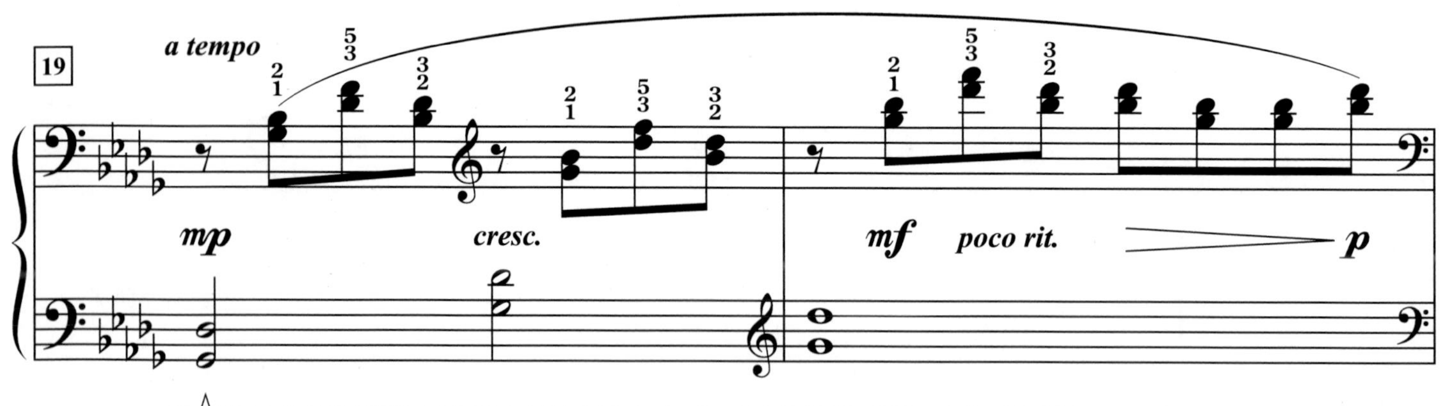
19
a tempo
mp
cresc.
mf
poco rit.
p

21
a tempo
mp
cresc.
mp
rit.
p
molto rit.
e dim.
pp

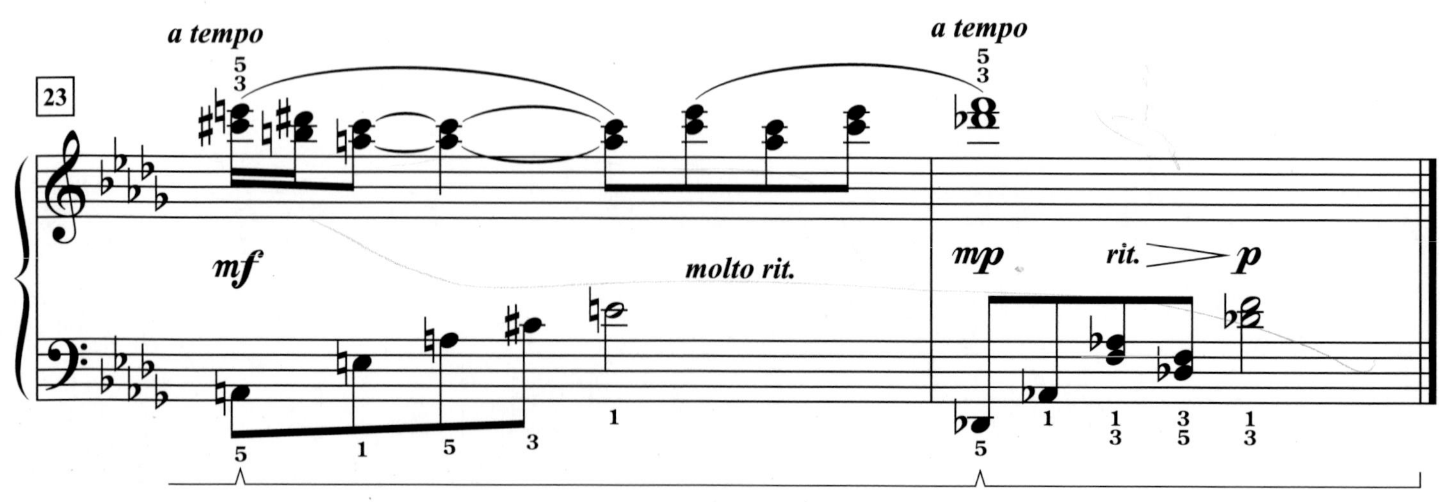
23
a tempo
mf
molto rit.
a tempo
mp
rit.
p

Valse Noble

Catherine Rollin

Impressionist Style

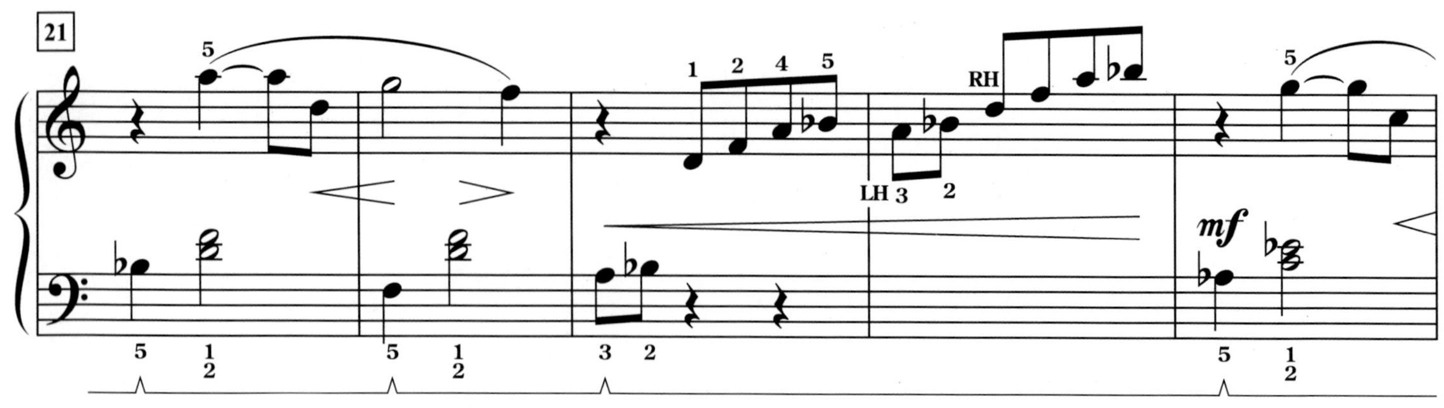
21
RH
LH
mf

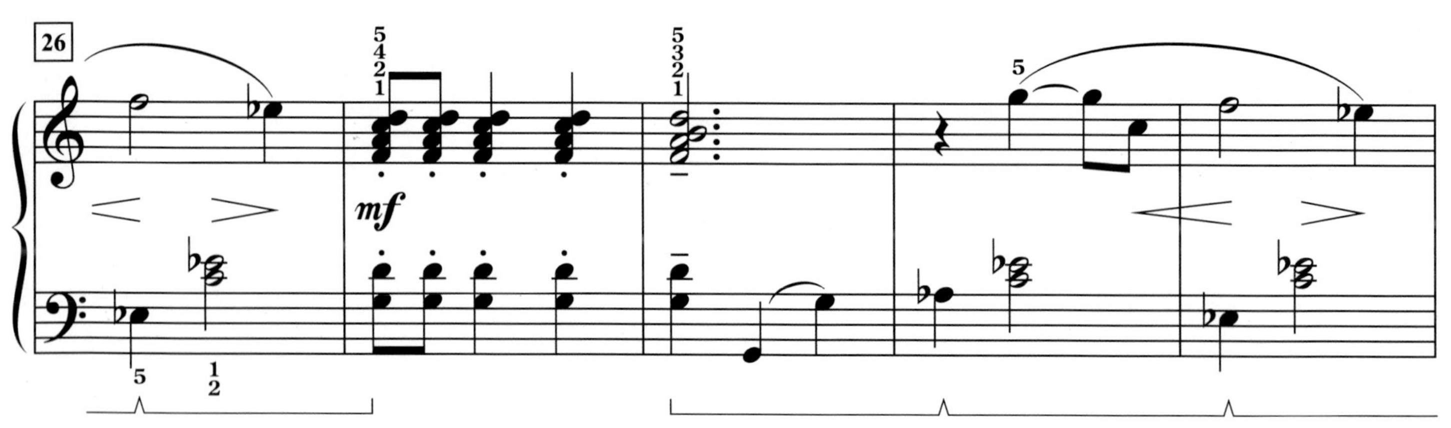
26
mf

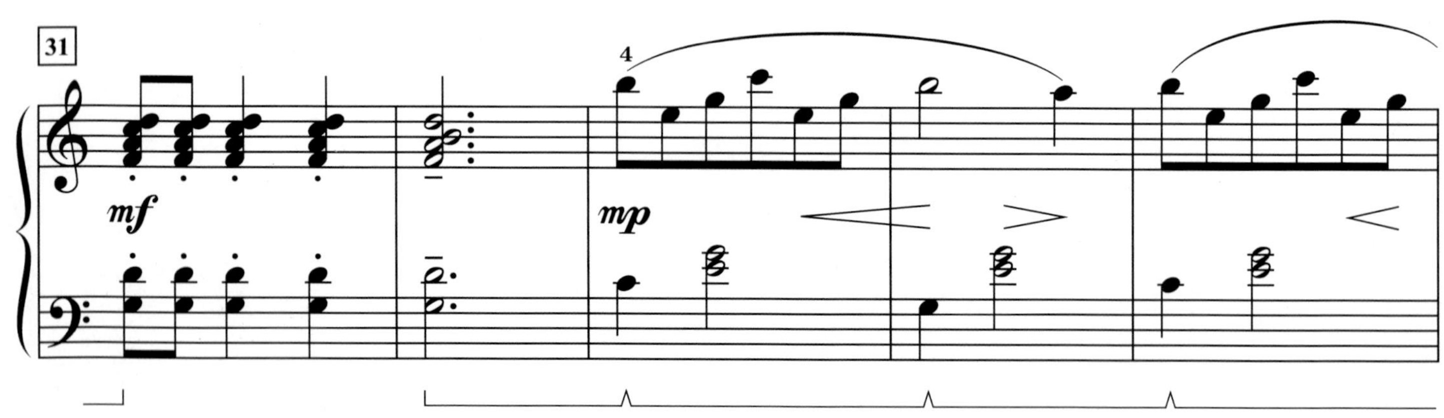
31
mf
mp

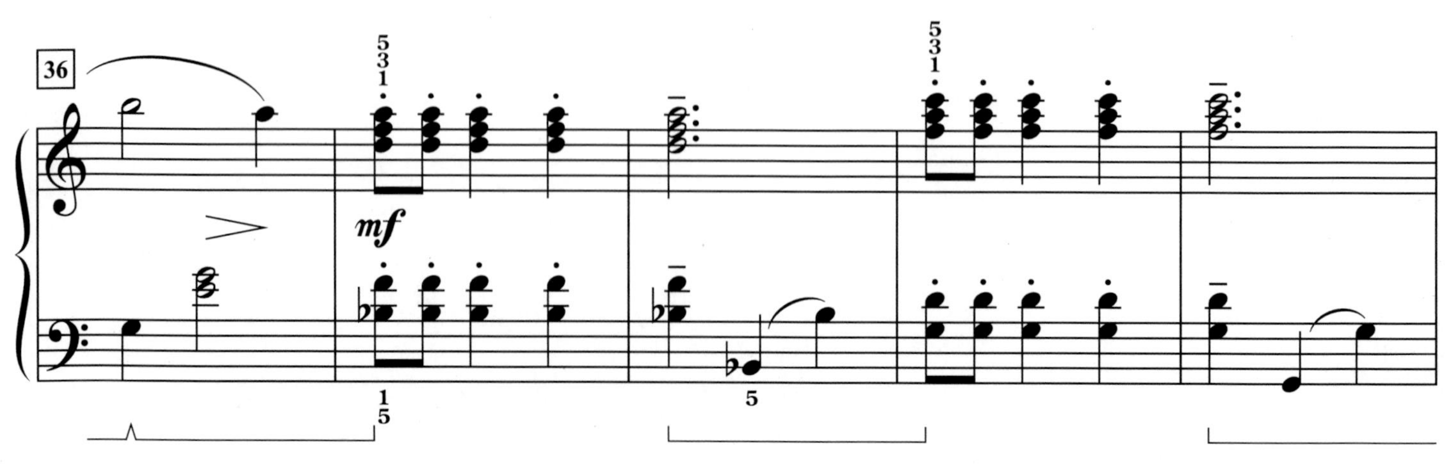
36
mf

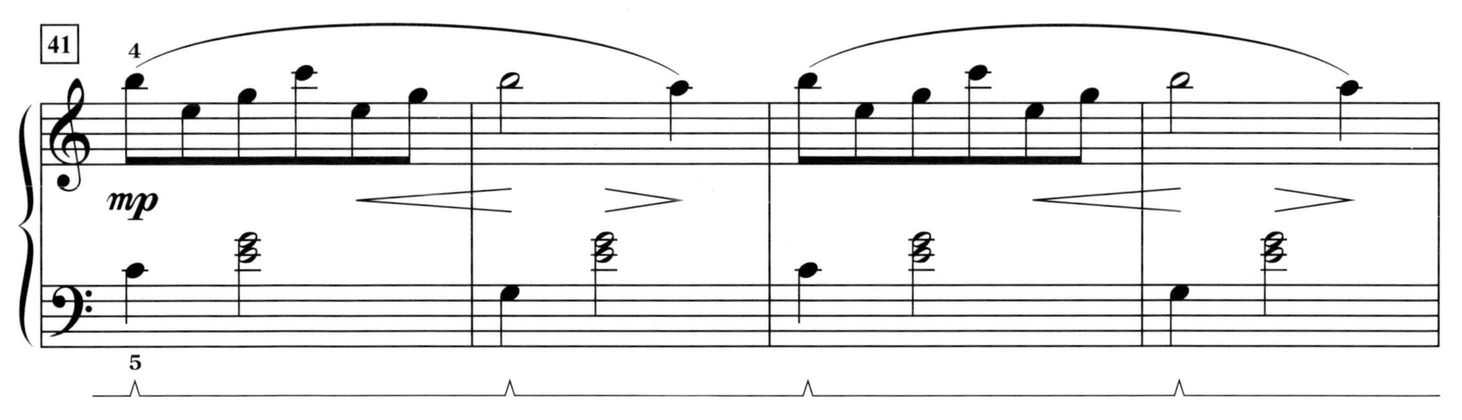
41
4
mp
5

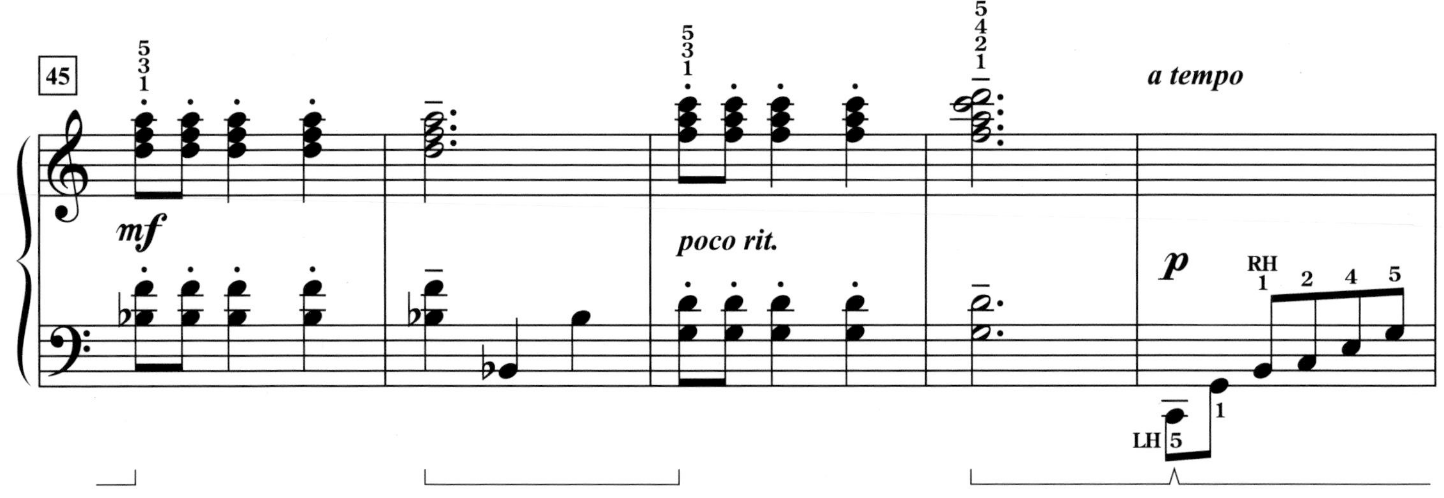
45
5
3
1
mf
poco rit.
5
4
2
1
a tempo
p
RH
1 2 4 5
LH 5
1

50
RH
1 2 4 5
cresc. poco a poco
LH 5 1
RH
1
LH 5
8va
RH
1
LH 5
4
2
1
mf
1
3
5

55
loco
RH
2 3 4
3 2 1
LH
8va
RH
2 3 4
3 2 1
LH
5
2
1
f
1
3
5
2
5
Both hands 8va lower

FOR SUMMER

VALSE SENTIMENTALE

CATHERINE ROLLIN

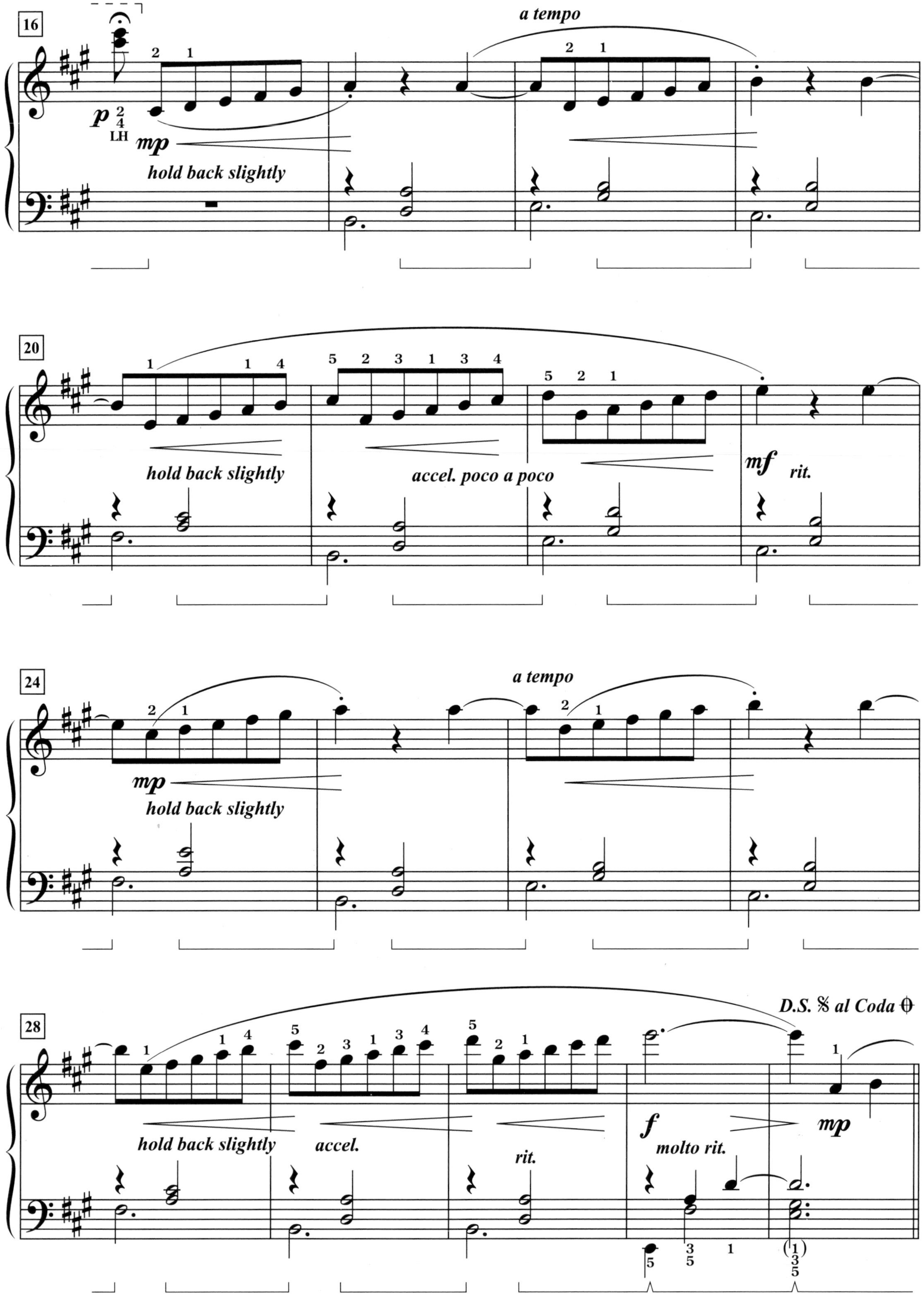

16
a tempo
p
mp
hold back slightly
20
hold back slightly
accel. poco a poco
mf
rit.
24
a tempo
mp
hold back slightly
28
D.S. 𝄋 al Coda 𝄌
hold back slightly
accel.
rit.
f
molto rit.
mp

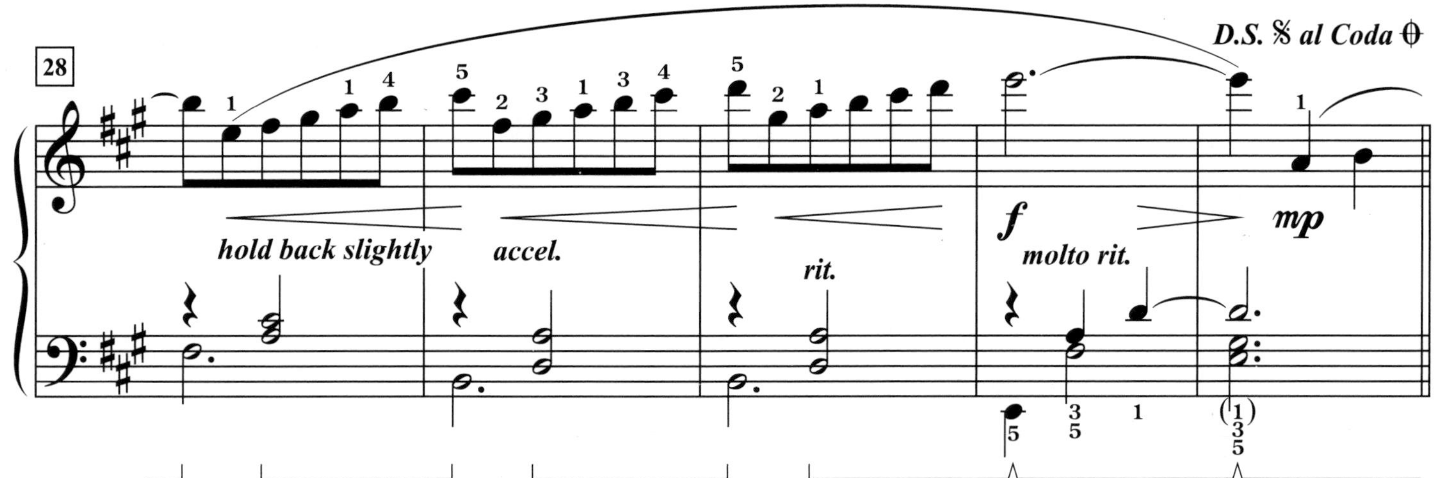

Coda
a tempo
1
p
2
4
LH
mp
hold back

37
a tempo
Both hands 8va higher
2
1
3
1
1
1
poco rit.
p
cresc. poco a poco
5
5
poco rit.
mf
5

41
a tempo
5
1
3
1
2
3
5
1
1
p
2
5
LH
mp
hold back
p
mp
rit.
5
5
5

45
a tempo
5
LH
mf
p
più rit.
mp
p
rit.
LH
mp
p
8va